Jacques A. Legrand, Henri Pène du Bois

Le Grand's Manual for Stamp Collectors

A companion to the stamp album - From the French of Dr. A. Le Grand

Jacques A. Legrand, Henri Pène du Bois

Le Grand's Manual for Stamp Collectors
A companion to the stamp album - From the French of Dr. A. Le Grand

ISBN/EAN: 9783337223014

Printed in Europe, USA, Canada, Australia, Japan

Cover: Foto ©Andreas Hilbeck / pixelio.de

More available books at **www.hansebooks.com**

LE GRAND'S
MANUAL FOR STAMP COLLECTORS

A COMPANION TO THE STAMP ALBUM

FROM THE FRENCH OF

DR. A. LE GRAND
(DR. MAGNUS)

Member of the Ethnographic Society, President of the New Society of Timbrology, and of the Committee of the Stamp Exhibition (1892), and of the Patrons (Timbrology Section) of the Book Exhibition (1894). Gold Medal (Hors Concours) 1892.

TRANSLATED, ADAPTED AND ANNOTATED FOR THE
AMERICAN COLLECTOR BY

HENRI PÈNE DU BOIS, Esq.

NEW YORK
GEORGE D. HURST, PUBLISHER

PREFACE.

This work is the result of thirty years of studies and researches. The science of it was at first for me only an amusement; it became gradually the subject of labors of all sorts, unrelated to my profession, but full of ever renewed pleasures. The collection of stamps is no longer a mania which one need defend. It requires intelligence for classification, skill and care in the arrangement of albums, and procures a great quantity of geographical, historical, ethnographic, linguistic, commercial and industrial information.

I have reunited in this series of chapters the phases of knowledge through which one passes in collecting stamps.

Dr. LEGRAND.

INTRODUCTION.

Origin of Timbrology.

"Timbrophilism," love of stamp collecting, is not ancient in the history of humanity, but it is more extensive than other varieties of love of collections. The various stamps used formerly as fiscal marks were gathered by rare amateurs, almost now unknown. The multiplicity of designs, their gracefulness and their delicacy pleased many persons; but postage stamps with their varied pictures and colors appealed to a much greater number. Still, there were few collectors in England and elsewhere until 1858. The mania originated in the public schools. It was encouraged because it made school children take interest in geography, history and foreign languages. At present the number of collectors is in the hundred thousands.

In France, in the public gardens every Sunday and Thursday, there were exchanges of postage stamps among pupils. The collections formed by Potiquet, Saulcy, Badin, Herpin, Donatis and Becourt, which have become famous, were formed in these childish meetings. France gave the first signal for the scientific development of timbrophilism.

The first catalogue of postage stamps was published by Potiquet in December, 1861. The following year Moens gave a manual of the stamp collector and Laplante another catalogue. In England Mount Brown, Gray, Booty, Stafford Smith, in 1862; Oppen in 1863, and Lincoln in 1864, published the first editions of their catalogues.

In Germany the catalogues of Zschiesche and Koeder, Beyfus, Priebatsch and Wuttig appeared in 1863, those of Mann, Jr., and Bauschke in 1864. In Switzerland. Wilhelm George's appeared in 1864 In the United States Kline's catalogue appeared in 1862. Since then the progress has been rapid. England published, in 1862, the first philatelist's journal, the "Stamp Collect. or's Review and Monthly Advertiser." France followed in 1863. I published in 1865, in " Le Timbrophile," my first essay on water-marks in stamps which had the honor of being reprinted in the English "Stamp Collector's Magazine" and in the American "Stamp Mercury." The United States, reasonably proud to-day of the quantity of catalogues and journals which they publish, came after Europe in chronological order and surpass them in quantity. In every city of the Union, almost, are many intelligent collectors. I have published in a stamp-collectors' journal of Belgium a communication from Mr. Tiffany, full of interesting details on the number of American publications relative to stamps. There were, in 1892, 762 journals and 692 catalogues. Add to these, price-lists, albums, directories of collectors and auction sale catalogues, and the total number of works reaches 17,399. It is only just to note the fortunate influence exercised by the publication of albums. In these the novice finds an easy method of classifying his collection.

The formation of societies has had an influence not less great. The Philatelic Society of London, founded in April, 1869, is the eldest ; the French Society of Timbrology is only twenty years of age. The most important society of Germany is that of Dresden, which is seventeen years of age and counts 1,553 members and 39 sections. Berlin. Munich, Stuttgart and all the principal cities of the German Empire have influential local societies. America has done this work on a large scale, as it does everything, for not content with having stamp clubs in a great number of towns, it possesses a grand federation of societies of stamp lovers. The aim of these societies may be divided into three classes : science, exchange and commerce. Some societies had no other reason for their foundation than to communicate the works and discoveries of their members, to examine them critically at meetings, and to publish them. The exchange societies desire above all to increase the number of stamps owned by their members. In these societies stamps circulate among the members freely, the society charging a small commission on every transaction. Merchants having taken advantage of this freedom are no longer agreeable members of such societies. In the commercial class there are no serious studies, there is only commerce. I think that societies should admit members of one only of the two categories, collectors and merchants. Evans, editor-in-chief of the "Monthly Journal," says truly that if a man becomes a member of a stamp society for amusement or for study he will do well ; but if he becomes a member of a scientific society for the purpose of making money he will do badly.

Vienna was the first city to give an exhibition of stamps. This occurred in 1881. Munich followed in 1884 and 1889, Dresden in 1886, Antwerp in 1887, New York in 1889, Amsterdam in 1889, Leeds in 1890, London in 1890, Vienna in 1890, Birmingham in 1891 and Stuttgart in 1892. London's exhibition was in two installments—one was at the Guildhall, in celebration of the fiftieth anniversary of the first postage stamp and was initiated by the Prince of Wales ; the second was opened by the Duke of Edinburgh as Honorary President of the Philatelic Society.

The development in the study of stamps during the last thirty years has made timbrology rival numismatics and sphragistics. Most people know that it was Herpin who created the words philately and philatelist to designate the science and the amateurs of postage stamp collection. These words are derived from two Greek words, "philos," friend, and "ateles," relative to an object free from all tax. Philately signifies love of all that relates to objects freed from tax. It was an error to give these terms to stamp collecting, for "ateles" expresses exemption from charges, gratuity. It has been said that the word timbrology is not as harmonious as philately, that it was barbarous since composed of a Greek word and of a word borrowed from another language. But if one consults Littré's dictionary one may verify that this word is derived from "tupto" and from "tumpanon," words which are incontestably Greek and easily allied with "philos" and "logos" that are of the same language. The word philately is not properly applied to the love for stamp collection when the stamps loved are postage stamps, and it should be rejected absolutely from the science of stamps which are not postal. The word is not used in France, but it is serviceable in England and America where the words "stamp," "label" and "ticket" may not be allied with "philos" and "logos." Timbrology and timbrologist do not sound ill in English. The Greek journals do not use "philately." I think that the word is inadequate, and will avoid it.

HOW THIS BOOK IS DIVIDED.

To tell with method all that concerns timbrology I shall divide the subject into three parts :

The first part will treat of stamps in general and successively, of all details concerning their issue.

The second part will treat of the various sorts of stamps, postal telegraphic and fiscal or revenue.

The third part will treat only of subjects relating to stamps not discussed in the two preceding parts—obliterations, surcharges, proofs, reprints, counterfeits, etc. An article on the Universal Postal Union and another on the formation of an album will finish this part.

FIRST PART.

ON STAMPS IN GENERAL—WHAT IS A STAMP?

The word "stamp" is applied to a great number of imprints giving an inscription or design. These chapters will explain only the stamps that present a receipt for a tax. The postage stamp is the best known type of the class. Therefore, all administrative stamps serving to indicate the origin of a document but not representing a receipt for a tax are not to be discussed here. There are real stamps which were impressed by hand. Some were used in the beginning of stamp issues, or were used as temporary stamps. Such are those of the first issue of Moldavia and those of Guadalajara. Others are used every day and represent a tax, as do the seals on newspapers. Following the example of the greater number of collectors, I shall discard these and consider only the stamps which necessitated a special manufacture.

The stamp representing a receipt for a tax has different aspects, according to the use which may be made of it and the way in which it is printed.

There are postal, telegraph or fiscal stamps. The latter have various names in various countries. In France there are stamps of dimensions, proportional stamps and fixed duty stamps. The first are subdivided into stamped paper stamps, used for deeds of notaries, and poster stamps, used for advertising bills. The charge of the dimension stamp is made according to the size of the paper and its use.

Proportional stamps are used for commercial documents. The tax is figured in proportion to the sum indicated on the document.

Fixed duties are determined by special laws regardless of the size of the paper and the value of the document. The receipt stamp is the most characteristic example of the fixed duty stamp.

Fiscal stamps in America, in England and in English colonies are called revenue stamps.

Telegraphic stamps are used for postage and telegrams. Such were issued recently by the Argentine Republic and are inscribed " Correos y Telegrafos."

English stamps of 1887 are marked " Postage and Revenue." This was an attempt to simplify stamp issues against which administrative routine, or the desire to verify the importance of the sources of public revenue, opposes a serious obstacle.

Postage stamps are the best known if they are not the most numerous. There are several varieties of them. Sometimes the stamp is printed in great number on sheets, afterward gummed, and every stamp is used by wetting the gum and affixing it on the letter or document which is to carry it. This variety of stamp is the movable stamp. Sometimes, on the contrary, the stamp is printed in advance on leaves or cards which serve as stamped envelopes, wrappers, postal cards and money orders. This variety of stamps is in the same order as stamped papers.

The latter have been in use in all countries since the origin of stamps.   In England drug stamps were wrappers with which bottles and drugs subject to revenue duty were capped.   This method of collecting revenue duties was probably made at the beginning of stamp issues, since I have in my collection a rectangular stamp similar to the drug stamps bearing on the circle surrounding the royal crown the words "Gloves, Duty Two Pence ;" on the sides, "Stamp Office ;" at the top, "Above 10d.," and at the bottom.   "Not Exceeding 1s. 4d."   Similar stamps may even have been used in England at an epoch preceding the use of postage stamps.

According to the manner in which they are printed, stamps may be distinguished as printed, engraved and lithographed.   I shall write of this later.

I have often heard the following observation : Stamp collecting is becoming more and more extensive and many collectors prefer to attach themselves to a single branch in order to collect examples of the smallest details and varieties.   One collector cares only for postage stamps, either movable or printed on wrappers, cards and envelopes.   Another prefers revenue stamps.   Other collectors want stamps of only one country, and gather all its examples of all kinds and epochs.   I understand and do not blame such collectors.   I approve the young amateur who limits himself to gathering a specimen of all the values of each series and of all the principal changes in color; who does not collect varieties of water-marks, nor errors, nor official reprints.   But I insist that the study of all these details is necessary, because it permits one to distinguish counterfeit stamps from good ones.   Study them if you do not wish to fill your albums with the counterfeits and imitations that

unscrupulous merchants only too often offer to your inexperience.

Must one collect new stamps or cancelled stamps?

Those who collect cancelled stamps often imagine that
the cancellation is a guarantee of authenticity. They
see in the cancellation a proof that the stamp was
bought at the post office, and that it is real. This is an
error. Nothing is easier to imitate than a cancellation.
A cork, a piece of wood engraved with some skillfulness ;
such is what gives authenticity to a stamp in the view of
many collectors. Is it not clear that the details of a
stamp, even when made by an ordinary artist, are much
more difficult to imitate than the design, always coarse,
of its cancellation ?

I do not deny that in certain cases cancellations may
have some utility; but, then, study of cancellations should
precede that of stamps. The question is not whether
the stamp was bought at the post office, but whether it
is authentic. New stamps sold by honest merchants
were bought at the post office. Since people have begun
to collect stamps, the collectors of every country or the
correspondents of stamp dealers have always sent to the
latter new issues of stamps as they were given out, with
the decrees or laws that announced their issue. Their
design is therefore perfectly authentic, and they do not
need to be cancelled in order to be genuine. Is not a
collection infinitely more beautiful when the stamps are
new, with fresh colors, with designs untarnished?

To give an idea of the small importance which should
be ascribed to cancellation, I recall a fact which occurred
twenty-five years ago. A collector who had bought a
certain number of new stamps of all countries, had taken
advantage of a post-clerk's kindness to have them all
cancelled with French seals. Judge of the authenticity

which French seals could give to English, Belgian, German, Italian or Spanish stamps ! It cannot be doubted that such vandalism has been often committed. At all events, counterfeit stamps are usually cancelled stamps.

An innovation, the use of which is due to Moens, permits one nowadays to recognize all the varieties of stamps composing a sheet, in countries where processes of a multiplication of a type of stamps are not yet well known. The "Catalogue Prix-Courant de Timbres-Poste," 7th edition, gives scrupulously faithful photographic plates. Nothing is easier than to verify by a rapid examination of these plates, the stamps belonging to one of the sheets, and this method is much more certain than the study of cancellations. Moens has rendered a signal service to collectors. Scott has followed Moens's example, and the Philatelic Society of London has reproduced by a different photographic process the Australian stamps in a book entitled "The Postage Stamps of Australia and the British Colonies of Oceanica."

Since cancellation cannot be regarded as a certificate of authenticity, it seems more reasonable to me to collect new stamps. But if this be preferable for the rich amateur, for the greater number it is impracticable. The greater number should collect the cleanest cancelled stamps, that is, stamps as little cancelled as possible, or bearing a surcharge precluding their use at the post office, or marked "Specimen," "Cancelled," "Probe," "Saggio," "Muestra," etc. Thus one may place in one's collection stamps of 10, 20, and more pesos, at a price which will not be prohibitive. What collector of revenue stamps would buy, at their face value, the series of Court Fee stamps of India, a series of twenty-four stamps valued at 2,564 rupees, or about $1,280? The series marked "Specimen" forms a collection superb enough.

Even the rich amateur would prefer to have a very rare stamp cancelled than not to have it at all in his album. To collect new or cancelled stamps is therefore a question of money. Place in your collection all the stamps that you may buy new; content yourself with all those that are difficult to find in any State. The wealth of a millionaire would not be sufficient to pay for all the varieties of stamps.

Place in your collections stamps as nearly as possible in the state in which they were when they were first issued. Cancelled or not, they should have their full margins if they are not perforated, and the notches if they are perforated. They should also retain the gum. If they have been used, take off the paper which adhered to the reverse of the stamp, but preserve the gum. Do not stick the stamps on your album, but mount them on strong paper, white, in order to make the colors on the stamps stand out. Avoid all washings and cleanings with soap or benzine, that alter the color and the strength of the paper. But we shall return to this question later.

In the following pages are details applicable not only to postage stamps, but to telegraphic and revenue stamps, which are made by the same processes, and often in the same establishments.

DESIGNS IN STAMPS.

The first question about a stamp concerns its origin. To what country does it belong? Two things tell this: the design and the legend. When the legend contains the name of the country in Roman characters nothing can be easier; but this seldom happens, and in most cases the design must suffice.

One must consider, in the design of a stamp, its general form in the first place. The rectangular form is the most common. There are square, round, oval, hexagonal and octagonal stamps. Others are irregular. The size of each one of these forms may vary. Some ancient postage stamps, like those of Brazil, are 27 by 29 millimetres in size. Movable postage stamps are usually rectangular, and their most common size is 19 by 23 millimetres. Telegraphic stamps are varied in size and form. The most ancient revenue stamps are rectangular and measure 22 by 58 millimetres.

There are two parts in the designs, the central part, which is the capital one, and the frame. I shall have little to say of the frame. In this the artist's fancy has its play. The frame contains all possible combinations of lines, is surcharged with ornaments, attributes, shields and, ordinarily, bears a legend.

The central part may belong to one of the four following classes :

1.—Portrait of the reigning prince, of an illustrious person, or an allegorical figure.

2.—Arms of the country or emblems.

3.—Value in figures.

4.—Legend.

As the following chapter is to treat of the legend on stamps, the reader will refer to this for the third and fourth classes.

The portrait of the reigning sovereign is one of the best means of verifying at first sight the country to which a stamp belongs. The portrait of Queen Victoria is on the greatest number of stamps in Great Britain. No movable stamp of Great Britain contains the name of the country.

Victoria

Tasmania

The queen's effigy appears on the stamps of the English colonies. The name of the colony is usually added to these stamps.

Among the stamps which do not bear the name of the country, but which may be recognized by the portrait of the sovereign may be named those of Austria, Lombardy, Hungary, with the portrait of Francis Joseph ; Belgium, with the portrait of Leopold I. ; Spain,

Francis-Joseph

Léopold I

with the portrait of Isabella until 1866, those of Amedus and Alfonso XII. since 1872, and of Alfonso XIII. ; of Piedmont with the portrait of Victor Emmanuel, since the formation of the Kingdom of Italy, on some revenue stamps ; Portugal until 1866 ;

Isabella

Amedeus

Prussia, with the portrait of William IV.; Cuba and the Phillipine Islands with Spanish portraits, the first until 1868, and the last until 1872 ; Persia.

Alfonso XII

Alfonso XIII

The presence of royal portraits on stamps is certainly a monument destined to perpetuate the memory of reigns. Even pretenders nowadays issue stamps before they coin money. The stamps of Don Carlos in Spain and those of Maximilian in Mexico are samples of this innovation.

Maximilian

Don Carlos

Prince of Wales

There are also in stamps portraits of members of royal families. Some Canadian stamps bear the portrait of the Prince of Wales, and some of those of Hawaii have portraits of princes and princesses.

Victor-Emmanuel

Nasser Eddin

Frederick-William IV

The stamps of the United States of America have the portraits of Washington, Franklin, Jefferson, Andrew Jackson, Lincoln and other great American personages. Jefferson Davis, Andrew Jackson and Calhoun have their portraits on the stamps of Confederate States.

| Jefferson Davis | Thomas Jefferson | Calhoun |

The Argentine Republic imitates the United States in this fashion. Its stamps have the portraits of Rivadavia, Belgrano, San Martino, Mitre, Moreno, Celman and others.

| Rivadavia | Belgrano | Martino |

Hayti stamps have the portrait of President Salomon ; portraits of generals appear on the stamps of Honduras, Costa Rica, Guatemala and Venezuela. Mexico has given on its stamps the portraits of its innumerable presidents, and Colombia has done likewise.

Salomon   Morazan   P. Fernandez

Heads of Liberty, wearing caps more or less Phrygian, graceful heads of Minerva or of the Republic, more or less fanciful, complete this gallery, which is as long as it is varied. Ordinarily the bust alone is represented.

There are portraits of Queen Victoria on her throne on stamps of the Victoria Colony. There are figures of Minerva or allegorical figures of Britannia on the stamps of Trinidad, Barbados and Mauritius.

The coats-of-arms and emblems are not less varied. To recognize them one should have some knowledge of heraldry. How could one otherwise find his way amongst so many lions and eagles? Western Australia assumes the swan, Peru the llama, Basle the dove, China the dragon, Bulgaria the lion, Japan the chrysanthemum. Some stamp dealers have had the ingenious idea of publishing sheets of colored coats of arms, which are useful.

Some emblems indicate the use to which stamps are to be put. There are winged wheels, postmen on horseback, and horns for the post office; lightning on telegraphic stamps; a caduceus on commercial stamps; justice and her scales on stamps employed by tribunals; a locomotive on stamps of railways and ocean lines.

On some stamps landscapes are printed. The American Bank Note Company issued the first stamps printed with views of Nicaragua, Costa Rica, Salvador. The reproduction of two paintings representing the landing of Christopher Columbus and the Declaration of Independence are especially to be noted. In 1893 the stamps of the Centennial of the discovery of America formed a series of small pictures. The Hamilton Bank Note Company has followed the example of the American Bank Note Company. Views of Sydney, pyramids of Egypt, and other pictures have delighted many collectors.

Animals and vegetables have also been figured on stamps. Stamps of Russia contain a great quantity of coats-of-arms. A curious variety is that of the private revenue stamps of the United States on matches, playing cards and drugs.

LEGENDS ON STAMPS.

The legend is the inscription which usually fills the frame of the stamp. When the legend is the principal part of the stamp it takes the form of an inscription, or of a tall figure indicating the value. The best known stamps of this variety are those of Hawaii. The stamps of Cashmere and of Hayderabad present a combination of words in two or four languages, accompanied in the first case with the Buddhic emblem, the lotus. A small number of serial stamps have no other design than the name of the country, the value, and typographical marks. Such are the temporary stamps of English Guiana, which bear also the signature of one of the post clerks.

The legend on stamps is ordinarily written in Roman characters, but there are many countries that use special alphabets, as Russia, Greece, Turkey, Persia, China and Japan. Every serious collector appreciates the necessity of knowing how to read these legends, or at least of knowing how to place the stamps in their correct classes.

There are four principal points in the legend on stamps :

1.—The name of the country.

2.—Indications of the use to which the stamps are put.

3.—The value expressed in figures or letters.

4.—The currency.

The name of the country needs to be explained only when notable differences make it difficult to recognize.

VALUE IN MONEY OF STAMPS.

The value of stamps may be expressed in figures or in letters. This chapter will refer only to the values expressed in Roman letters. These are in one of the following languages :

German, French, Danish, Spanish, Finnish, Dutch, Hungarian, Italian, Portugese, Romanian, Swedish, Hawaiian.

In the enumeration which follows I have given all the numbers, from one to twenty, in their natural order. Then the names which express their values in round numbers, from twenty to one hundred. I give also a summary of the rules for the formation of intermediary numbers, with some examples.

GERMAN.

1, Ein ; 2, zwei ; 3, drei ; 4, vier ; 5, funf; 6, sechs ; 7, sieben ; 8, acht; 9, neun ; 10, zehn ; 11, eilf; 12, zwoelf; 13, dreizehn ; 14, vierzhen ; 15, funfzehn ; 16, sechzehn ; 17, siebenzehn ; 18, achtehn ; 19, neunzehn ; 20, zwanzig ; 30, dreissig ; 40, vierzig ; 50, funfzig ; 60, sechzig ; 70, siebenzig ; 80, achtzig ; 90, neunzig ; 100, hundert ; 1.000, tausend.

The intermediary numbers in decimals are expressed by the number of the unities and the number of the decimals united by the word und. Thus 25 is expressed by funf und zwanzig.

For hundreds the multiples are placed before the word hundert ; 300, drei hundert. Unities are placed afterward ; 103, ein hundert und drei.

Principal fractions : ½, ein halder ; 1-3, ein drittel ; ¼, ein viertel.

COUNTRIES THAT USE GERMAN.

Prussia, Oldenburg, Mechlinburg, Hamburg, Bergedorf, Bremen, Hanover, Brunswick, Saxony, Baden, Bavaria, Wurtemburg, Austria, and in general all the countries which form part of the ancient Germanic Confederation.

FRENCH.

1, un; 2, deux; 3, trois; 4, quatre ; 5, cinq; 6, six ; 7, sept; 8, huit; 9, neuf; 10, dix ; 11, onze ; 12, douze ; 13,

treize; 14, quatorze; 15, quinze ; 16, seize ; 17, dix-sept ;
18, dix-huit ; 19, dix-neuf; 20, vingt ; 30, trente ; 40, qua-
rante; 50, cinquante; 60, soixante ; 70, soixante-dix ; 80,
quatre-vingts ; 90, quatre-vingts-dix ; 100, cent ; 1,000,
mille.

Intermediary values from twenty to one hundred are
formed by adding unities after the number of decimals :
24, vingt-quatre; 72, soixante-douze.

The multiples of one hundred are formed by placing
the number before the word cent : 300, trois cents.

Principal fractions : ½, une demie ; 1-3, un troisieme,
or un tiers; ¼, un quart.

COUNTRIES THAT USE FRENCH.

France and its colonies.

DANISH.

1, een; 2, to; 3, tre; 4, fire; 5, fem; 6, sex; 7, syv; 8,
otto; 9, ni; 10, t i; 11, elleve ; 12, tolv ; 13, tretten ; 14,
fierten; 15, temten; 16, sexten; 17, setten; 18, atten; 19,
nitten ; 20, tyve ; 30, tredive ; 40, fyrgetive ; 50, halv-
tredsindstyne ; 60, tredsinds tyve ; 70, halvfjersindstyve ;
80, firsindstyve ; 90, holvlemsindstyve ; 100, hundrede ;
1,000, tusinde.

In compound numbers the smaller precedes the
greater: 22 is expressed by to og tyve. To abbreviate,
people say fyrre for forty.

Principal fractions : ½, een halv : 1-3, een trediedeel ;
¼, een fierdedeel.

COUNTRIES THAT USE DANISH.

Denmark, Norway, Iceland, Dutch India, Danish
West Indies.

The Norwegian language is only a dialect of the
Danish, yet there is a difference in the manner of expressing certain numbers, as follows:

50, femti; 60, sexti; 70, syvti; 80, otti; 90, niti.

SPANISH.

1, uno ; 2, dos ; 3, tres ; 4, cuatro; 5, cinco ; 6, seis; 7, siete; 8, ocho; 9, neuve; 10, diez; 11, once; 12, doce; 13, trece ; 14, catorce ; 15, quince ; 16, diez y seis ; 17, diez y siete ; 18, diez y ocho ; 19, diez y nueve ; 20, veinte ; 30, treinta ; 40, cuarenta ; 50, cincuenta ; 60, sesanta ; 70, setenta; 80, ochenta ; 90, noventa; 100, cien et ciento; 1,000, mil.

The intermediary values from 16 to 100 are formed by placing first the number of decimals, then adding that of the unities and uniting them with the conjunction "y," which means and.

Multiples of 100 are formed by placing the number before ciento, and making this word agree in gender and in number with the following noun : 300, tresciento or trescientas.

The word mil takes the mark of the plural like the nouns : 2000, dos miles.

The principal fractions: ½, medio ; 1-3, tercero ; ¼, cuarto.

COUNTRIES THAT USE SPANISH.

Spain, Phillipine Islands, Spanish West Indies, Cuba, Porto Rico, and the ancient American possessions of Spain.

FINNISH.

Finnish is found exclusively in the stamps of Finland, postal and revenue, concurrently with Swedish and, in later years, with Russian.

1, iksi ; 2, kaksi ; 3, kolme ; 4, neljoe ; 5, vusi ; 6, kuusi ; 7, seitseman ; 8, kahdelsan ; 9, yhdeksen ; 10, kymmenen ; 11, yksitoiska ; 12, kaksitoista ; 13, kolmetoista ; 14, neljaetoista ; 15, vusitoista ; 16, kinsitoista ;

17, seitsemantoista ;   18, kahdelsantoista ; 19, ykdeksen-
toista ; 20, kaksi kymmenta ; 30, kolme kymmenta ; 40,
neljo kymmenta ; 50, vusi kymmenta; 60 kuusi kymenta;
70, seitseman kymmenta; 80, kadeksan kymmenta; 90,
yhdeksen kymmenta ; 100, sata ; 1000, tuhatta.

I could not indicate in what manner are formed intermediary values from 20 to 100.

COUNTRIES THAT USE FINNISH.

Besides Finland: Russian, Sweedish and Norwegian
Lapland.

DUTCH.

1, een ; 2, twee ; 3, drie ;   4, vier ;   5, vijf ;   6, zes ; 7,
zeven ; 8, acht ; 9, negen ; 10, tien ; 11, elf ; 12, twaalf ;
13, dertien ;   14, veertien ;   15, vijftien ; 16, zestien ; 17,
zeventien ;   18, achtien ;   19, negentien ;   20, twingtig ;
30, dertig ; 40, veertig ; 50, vijftig ; 60, zestig ; 70, zeven-
tig ; 80, achtig ; 90, negentig ; 100, hunderd ; 1000, du-
izend.

Intermediary numbers are formed as in German.

Principal fractions: $\frac{1}{2}$, een half ; 1-3, een derde ; $\frac{1}{4}$,
vierendeel.

COUNTRIES THAT USE DUTCH.

The Netherlands and colonies, Curacoa and Surinam.
In Africa : Republics of Orange and of the Transvaal.

HUNGARIAN.

1, egy ; 2, ket ; 3, harom ; 4, negy ; 5, ot ; 6, hat ; 7,
het ; 8, nyolcz ; 9, kilencz ; 10, tiz ; 11, tizenegy ; 12,
tizenket ; 13, tizenharom ; 14, tizennegy ; 15, tizenot ;
16, tizenhat ; 17, tizenhet ; 18, tizennyolcz ; 19, tizenki-
lencz ; 20, husz ; 30, harmincz ; 40, negyven ; 50, ot-
ven ; 60, hatven ; 70, hetven ; 80, nyolczven ; 90, kilen-
czven ; 100, szaz ; 1000, ezer.

Intermediary values are formed by placing unities after

decimals : 36, harminz hat, and by making additions and corrections which it would take too long to explain.

Principal fractions: ½, egy fel ; 1-3, egy harmad ; ¼, egy negyed.

Countries that use Hungarian.

Hungary and countries of the Austrian Empire beyond the Leitha.

Italian.

1, un, uno una ; 2, due ; 3, tre ; 4, quattro ; 5, cinque ; 6, sei ; 7, sette ; 8, otto ; 9, nove ; 10, dieci ; 11, undici ; 12, dodici ; 13, tredici ; 14, quattordici ; 15, quindici ; 16, sedici ; 17, dieci sette ou diciasette ; 18, dieci otto ou diciotto ; 19, dieci nove ou diciannovo ; 20, venti ; 30, trenta ; 40, quaranta ; 50, cinquanta ; 60, sessanta ; 70 settanta ; 80, ottanta ; 90, novanta ; 100, cento ; 1000, mille.

The intermediary numbers from 20 to 100 are formed by placing the unity after the decimal : 25, venti cinque. Suppress the I or the A with the uno ; 21 vent-uno.

The number which expresses a multiple of 100 or 1000 is placed in front ; 300 trecento ; 2000, due mila, while 1200 and other analogous numbers are translated by mille et duecento.

Principal fractions: ½, mezzo ; 1-3, terso ; ¼, quarto.

Countries that use Italian.

Kingdom of Italy and former States by which it was formed.

Republic of San Marino;

Illyrian provinces of the Austro-Hungarian Empire.

Portuguese.

1, hum or um (masculine), huma, uma (feminine); 2, dois or dous (m), duas (f); 3, tres; 4, quatro ; 5, cinco ; 6, seis ; 7, sete or sette ; 8, oito or onto ; 9, nove ; 10, dez; 11, onze; 12, doze; 13. treze; 14, quatorze; 15, quinze; 16, dezeseis; 17, dezesete; 18, dezoito; 19, dezanove; 20, vinte; 30, trinta; 40, quarenta; 50, cincoenta; 60, sessanta; 70, setenta; 80, oitenta; 90, noventa; 100, cem or cento; 1000, mil.

Intermediary numbers from 20 to 200 are expressed by placing the number of decimals before that of the units.

The multiples of 100 are expressed by placing the multiple before the word centos or centas, except 200, duzentos; 300, trezentos, and 500, quinhentos.

Principal fractions: ½, meio, meia; 1-3, tercero, tercera; ¼, quarto, quarta.

Countries that use Portuguese.

Portugal and its colonies, Brazil.

Roumanian.

1, unu, una; 2, doui, doue; 3, trei; 4, patru; 5, cinci; 6, sese; 7, septe; 8, optu; 9, noue; 10, dece; 11, un -spre-dece; 12, doui-spre-dece; 13, trei spre-dece; 14, patru-spre-dece; 15, cinci-spre-dece; 16, sese-spre-dece; 17, septe-spre-dece; 18, optu-spre-dece; 19, noue-spre-dece; 20, doue-deci; 30, trei-deci; 40, patru-deci; 50, cinci-deci; 60, sese-deci; 70, septe-deci; 80, optu-deci; 90, noue-deci; 100, o suta; 1000. o mia.

Intermediary numbers from 20 to 100 are formed by placing the number of decimals followed by that of units, united by the conjunction si; 25, doue deci si cinci; 100, suta, and 1000, mia, are in the plural, sute and mii.

Principal fractions, ½, diumetate; 1-3, o treime; ¼, o patrime.

Countries that use Roumanian.

Roumania.

Swedish.

1, en; 2, tva; 3, tre 4, fyra; 5, fem; 6, sex; 7, sju;

8, atta ; 9, nie ; 10, tie ; 11, elfva ; 12, tolf ; 13, tretton ; 14, fjorton ; 15, femton ; 16, sexton ; 17, sjutton ; 18, aderton ; 19, nitton ; 20, tjugo ; 30, tretio ; 40, fyrtio ; 50, femtio ; 60, sextio ; 70, sjutio ; 80, attio ; 90, nitio ; 100, hundrade ; 1000, tusende.

Intermediary values from 20 to 100 are formed by placing units after decimals : 24, tjugo fyra.

Multiples of 100 or 1000 are obtained by placing the name of the multiple in front ; 200, tva hundrade.

Principal fractions: ½, half; 1-3, tredje ; ¼ , quarter.

COUNTRIES THAT USE SWEDISH.

Sweden and Finland.

HAWAIAN.

1, akahi ; 2, elua ; 3, ekolu ; 4, eha; 5, elima; 6, eono; 7, ekihu; 8, ewalu ; 9, eiwa ; 10, umi ; 11, umi kuman akahi ; 12, umi kuman elua ; 13, umi kumam akolu ; 14, umi kumam aha ; 15, uni kumam alima; 16, uni kuma aono ; 17, umi kumam akihu ; 18, umi kumam awalu; 19, umi kumam aiwa ; 20, eiwa kalua ; 30, kana kolu ; 40, kanaha ; 50, kanalima ; 60, kan aono ; 70, kan akihu ; 80, kanawalu ; 90, kanaiva ; 100, kanahumi.

I could not indicate how intermediary values from 20 to 1000 are formed.

Principal fractions: ½, hapalua ; 1-3 hapakolu ; ¼, hapaha.

COUNTRIES THAT USE HAWAIAN.

All the islands of the Hawaian kingdom.

NOMENCLATURE OF MONEYS.

FRANCE.

The unit is a silver franc which weighs five grammes at 835 / 1000. The multiples and divisions of the franc are of proportional weight. The weight of a five-franc piece is 25 grammes at 900 / 1000.

The other multiples of the franc are in gold at 900 / 1000.

Copper coins weigh one gramme per centime.

Since 1866, there is a monetary convention between France, Belgium, Italy, Switzerland and Greece. Their coins have the same weight. The agreement relates to copper coins only.

The values on stamps of French colonies are identical with those of the metropolis. There is only one small exception in the revenue stamps of French India.

GREAT BRITAIN.

The unit is the gold soverign or pound. It is equivalent to $4.84, and is expressed by the sign £.

There are twenty shillings in the pound.

A shilling equals twelve pence, equals twenty-five cents.

One penny equals two cents.

A half-penny equals one cent.

There are other moneys on ancient stamps not of postal origin.

One crown equals five shillings, equals $1.25.

Half crown equals 2 shillings and 6 pence, equals 63 cents.

One farthing equals one-quarter penny.

BELGIUM.

As in France.

LUXEMBURG.

There are francs and centimes of the same value as in France, but Luxemburg is not a part of the monetary union. Among the first issue of stamps is one valued at one silbergros, which equals a half cent, as in the Germanic Confederation.

NETHERLANDS.

The florin or gulden equals 42 cents. It is divided into one hundred cents or hundreths of florin.

GERMAN EMPIRE.

Since January 1873, Germany counts by Reichmarks. One Reichmark equals 25 cents. It is divided into one hundred pfenni gs. The several countries which constitute the Empire of Germany formerly had special moneys.

PRUSSIA.

The Prussian thaler equals 75 cents, and is divided into 30 silbergroschen, which equals 360 pfennigs.

HANOVER.

The thaler equals 75 cents, equals 30 groschen.
One groschen equals 10 pfennigs.

HAMBURG.

The mark banco equals 37 cents, and is divided into 16 shillings.
One shilling equals about 2 cents.
The mark equals 30 cents, equals 16 shillings.

LUBECK.

As at Hamburg.

BREMEN.

One thaler equals 72 grote, equals 83 cents.

SAXONY.

The thaler equals 72 cents, divided into 30 neugroschen, equals 300 pfennigs.

SOUTHERN GERMANY.

One florin or gulden equals 43 cents, equals 60 kreuzer. One kreuzer equals 70 cents.
In 1857, a monetary union thaler was established, the

value of which is 74 cents, divided into 100 kreuzer, the value of which remains even.

BADEN.

The florin equals 60 kreuzer, equals 42 cents.
Since 1857 the union thaler equals 74 cents.

BAVARIA.

Former accounts were rendered into florins of 60 kreuzers, equivalent to 42 cents.
At present the marks of Germany are in use.

WURTEMBURG.

The coins were those of Southern Germany, florins and kreuzer.
They are now reichmarks and pfennigs.

DENMARK.

In 1851, when the first postal stamps were issued, there were rigsbanks skillings.
One rigsbank daleror rixdaler equals 96 skillings, equals 56 cents.
In 1875, after the monetary union with Sweden and Norway, current money became :
The krome, equals 100 oere, equals 29 cents.

SCHLESWIG-HOLSTEIN.

The stamps of 1850 are in shillings like those of Hamburg.
One mark equals 16 shillings, equals 37 cents.
The first stamps of 1864 were in Danish skillings. They have been replaced by the current shillings of Hamburg.
The 1¼ shilling of 1864 bears the initials L. M.: Lauenburg Munz (Lauenburg money). The use of these stamps ceased January 1st, 1868.

SWEDEN.

The first issue was according to the ancient monetary system.

One rigsdaler equals 48 shillings, equals $1.14.

NORWAY.

The first issues were in skillings. The highest values of the Sportel Maerke are figured in skillings.

120 skillings equals $1.12.

ICELAND.

The moneys in use is that of Denmark.

FINLAND.

The first stamps are in kopecks and rubles.

One ruble equals 100 kopecks, equals 78 cents.

Since 1866 there are pennis and marks.

One mark equals 100 pennis, equal 20 cents.

RUSSIA.

The silver ruble is worth about 80 cents.

It is divided into 100 kopecks.

POLAND.

The stamps of the ancient kingdom are in Russian kopecks.

AUSTRIA-HUNGARY.

The ancient florin of Austria equals 60 kreuzer, equals 52 cents.

Since 1858 the new florin or gulden equals 100 kreuzer, equals 49 cents.

In Hungary the florin has the same value, and isknown as forint.

MONTENEGRO, BOSNIA AND HERZEGOVINA.

One florin equals 100 novtch, equals 50 cents.

SERVIA.

Turkish money was used at first. Since 1881 the dinar is the unit. It is worth 20 cents, and is divided into 100 paras.

MOLDAVIA, ROUMANIA.

Since 1868 the French monetary system has been adopted.

The ley equals 100 bani, equals 20 cents.

BULGARIA.

The first issue in stamps was in Turkish money. Later the French monetary system was adopted, but the franc and the centimes, which were inscribed at first on the stamps. were replaced by the lion and the stotinki of corresponding value.

TURKEY.

The Turkish pound equals 100 piastres, equals $4.50.

The Turkish piastre is currently in use for 5 cents. It is divided into 40 paras.

The foreign post offices established in Turkey surcharged their national stamps with paras and piastres.

France—25 centimes equals 1 piastre.

50	"	". 2	"
75	"	" 3	"
1 franc		" 4	"
5	"	" 20	"

Great Britain—2½ pence equals 40 paras.

5	"	"	80	"
2 sh. 6	"	"	12	piastres.

Germany—5 pfennig " 10 paras.

10	"	"	20	"
20	"	"	1	piastre.
25	"	"	1	" ¼.
50	"	"	2	" ½.

Austria—3 Kreutzer equals 20 paras.
       5   "   "   20   "
      10   "   "   1 piastre.
      20   "   "   2   "
      50   "   "   10   "

CYPRUS.

The money in use is that of Turkey and England.

GREECE.

The drachm equals 100 lepta, equals 20 cents.

IONIAN ISLANDS.

Before annexation to Greece the value was not printed on the stamps. Their cost was one, two and four obolus.

100 obolus equals $1.50.

MALTA.

English money is used.

ITALY.

The money now in use is the lire, equals 100 centesimi, equals 20 cents.

The various states that form the kingdom had formerly special coins.

PIEDMONT, PARMA, MODENA.

These states use the lire and centesimi.

TUSCANY.

The stamps of the ancient Duchy have the following values:
      1 quattrino equals cent. 1.4.
      1 soldo equals centime 4.2.
      1 crazie equals cent. 7.
      20 soldi formed the ancient Tuscan lire, the value of which was 17 cents.

ROMAN STATES.

The first issue of stamps were marked with the ancient values.

1 scudo equals 100 bajoques, equals $1.04.

The second issue of stamps is in centesimi.

TWO-SICILIES.

The issues for Naples and Sicily are in grani and in fractions of ducats.

1 ducat equals 100 grani, equals 84 cents.

SAN MARINO.

The money is that of Italy.

SWITZERLAND.

The law of 1850 abolished all moneys in use in order to adopt the French monetary system. The monetary union in 1866 confirmed this law. All moneys prior to 1860 have been withdrawn from circulation. The values are expressed in francs and rappen or centimes.

Before 1850, the various cantons had various moneys.

At Basle:

1 franken equals 10 batzen, equals 100 rappen, equals 30 cents. BERNE.

1 franken equals 10 batzen, equals 100 rappens, equals 22 cents.

At Geneva:

1 ancient pound equals 20 sous, equals 33 cents.

At Zurich:

1 florin equals 60 kreuzer or rappen, equals 47 cents.

MOROCCO.

The money used is the French money.

SPAIN.

At the beginning there were cuartos and reales.

1 duro equals 20 reales, equals $1.06.

1 real equals 5.2 cents.

The quarto is divided into four maraedis, money marked only on the Carlos stamps.

The division of the real is purely nominal; yet it is applied on stamps of commerce from 1863 to 1865.

PORTUGAL.

10 reis equals 1 cent.
50 reis equals v cents.
100 reis equals 10 cents.
200 reis equals 20 cents.
100c reis equals $1.00.

PORTUGUESE COLONIES.

The Portuguese Colonies use Portuguese values. Surcharges on stamps of the Azores and Madeira are to facilitate the control over the use of stamps at local post-offices.

EGYPT.

The piastre equals 5 cents. It is divided as in Turkey into 40 paras. The Suez Canal managers issued for a time stamps the value of which was expressed in centimes.

TUNIS.

The values are in francs and centimes.

ENGLISH COLONIES IN AFRICA.

The greater number figure in pence, shillings and pounds. In Eastern Africa the value of stamps is in annas and rupees.

FERNANDO PO .

The values are expressed in Spanish money.

LIBERIA.

United States money.

Mauritius.

The first issues were expressed in English money. Since January 1st, 1878, the figures are in rupees and hundredth of rupees.

1 rupee equals 48 cents.

Persia.

The toman equals 10 krans—equals $2.10.
The kran equals 20 shahis—equals 20 cents.

Bokkhara.

In spite of the doubts expressed about the stamps of that country, doubts that I do not share, I will indicate the value inscribed on those stamps.

The puls equals a 0.28.
Fifty puls equals 1 tanga—equals 14 cents.

Afghanistan.

The rupee is worth about 50 cents, divided into 16 shahis, or 8 sunar, or 4 abasy.

English India.

The rupee equals 50 cents, divided into 16 annas.

All the states of India express the values of their stamps in annas and rupees, except Nowanugger, which figures in docras, and Travancore, which figures in chuckram.

Ceylon.

Until 1872 the money expressed on stamps was English money. Since 1872 the rupee has been used.

Portuguese India.

The reis and its multiples have the same value as in the metropolis.

French India.

The fanam equals 6 cents.

MALACCA.

The money is the dollar, equals $1.

SIAM.

The bat or tical equals 60 cents. It is divided into four salungs, equals 8 fuangs, equals 16 seeks, equals 36 seos, equals 64 atts, equals 128 solots.

The postoffice of Bangkok uses Malacca stamps with a simple initial B. as a surcharge.

MACAO.

Uses Portuguese money.

SHANGHAI.

The candareen equals 1.5 cent.

1 tael equals 100 candareens, equals $1 at Canton.

The tael of Shanghai is worth much less than that of Canton.

1 tsien equals 15 cents.

In April, 1877, the values were expressed in cash.

1 tael equals 1,000 cash, equals $1.

HONG KONG.

Values are expressed in American dollars and cents. $1 equals 100 cents.

COREA.

Values are indicated in muns.

JAPAN.

1 yen equals $1.

DUTCH INDIES.

The money used is Dutch money.

PHILLIPINE ISLANDS.

The cuarto has the same value as in Spain.

HAWAII.

All values are expressed in cents and dollars, as in the United States. The name of the dollar is kala.

SARAW AK, NORTH BORNEO, LABUAN.

Values are expressed in dollars and cents.

AUSTRALIAN COLONIES.

All use the English money.

COLUMBIA AND VANCOUVER.

The first stamps were in pence.

The series of 1868 is in cents and dollars, as in the United States.

CANADA.

The first issue was in pence, the following were in cents.

The Dominion uses cents and dollars.

New Brunswick, Nova Scotia and Prince Edward Island used pence at first and cents afterward.

New Foundland did likewise.

UNITED STATES.

The American dollar equals 100 cents.

MEXICO.

The peso equals 8 silver reales, equals $1.

Under the Empire the decimal system was adopted and stamps bore their value in centavos.

GUATEMALA.

The peso has the value of the dollar, which equals 100 cents.

SALVADOR, NICARAGUA, COSTA RICA.

Same values as Guatemala.

HONDURAS.

Same monetary values.

BRITISH HONDURAS.

The first issues had their values expressed in English money, the following ones in cents.

$1 equals 100 cents.

ENGLISH WEST INDIES.

English money is used.

HAYTI.

The value of stamps is expressed in centavos. On revenue stamps the values is expresssed in gourdes.

One gourde equals $1.

SAN DOMINGO.

One piastre equals 100 centavos, equals $1.

The first stamps were in reales plata of the Spanish colonies.

CUBA, PORTO RICO.

The money used on the first stamps was the reale plata. One peso equals 8 reales, equals $1.

In 1866 the value was expressed in hundreds of piastres.

In 1871 the pesta equals 20 cents.

In 1881 the peso replaced the peseta.

FRENCH WEST INDIES.

The moneys used are those of France.

DANISH WEST INDIES.

One florin equals 42 cents.

CURACAO, SURINAM.

The money used is that of the Netherlands.

BRITISH GUIANA.

The dollar equals 100 centavos, equals $1.

VENEZUELA.

The first stamps issue was expressed in reales.

One real equals 13 cents.

The bolivar forms a fifth part of the venezolano, equals 20 cents.

ECUADOR.

The first issues were in reales, fractions of the piastre
1 ancient piastre equals 8 reales, equals 88 cents.
1 real equals 11 cents.

Since 1856 the piastre or sucre, the value of which is
$1, has been divided in accordance to the decimal
system.

BRAZIL.

The reis and its multiples have only half the value of
the Portuguese real.   The values which one finds habitually on Brazilian stamps are :
10 reis equals 0.45
50 reis equals 2.22 cents.
100 reis equals 5 cents.
1,000 reis equals 52 cents.
The highest value found on revenue stamps is :
50,000 reis equals $26.

COLOMBIA.

The peso has the weight and value of the French five
franc piece.

PERU.

The ancient peso of Peru was worth $1.   The peseta
formed the fifth part of it.   The dinero was a tenth of it.
By the law of January 31st, 1863, the monetary system
has been copied from that of France.   One sol equals
100 centavos, equals $1.

BOLIVIA.

The Bolivian piastre equals 100 centavos, equals $1.

PARAGUAY.

The piastre equals 100 centavos, equals $1.

The silver piastre has the same value and weight as the French five-franc piece.

ARGENTINE REPUBLIC.

The peso of the first issues was a silver peso worth about 78 cents.

URUGUAY.

The first issues are in centavos or hundredths of real.

1 real equals 11 cents. The peso is equal to 86 cents. This money was current until 1864.

1 peso equals 100 centesimos, equals $1.

BUENOS AYRES.

Formerly there was a silver peso, but its value was 4 cents only

THE MAKING OF PLATES.

The plate from which stamps are printed has three different aspects. The engraving may be in relief, on a plane surface or sunk. To these three states correspond three methods of printing, but I shall have to explain the mode of preparing the plate in order to make clearer the system of printing.

In the first process, after photographing the stamp design on the plate, and drawing all its details on the plate, which has been covered with varnish, the metal is dug out with a graver. Only the white parts of the plate are untouched.

Sometimes the lines are engraved in the varnish to the surface of the metal, which remains uncovered in the corresponding points. An acid is thrown on the plate, which fils the sections of the varnish and penetrates to the metal. When the acid has produced its effect, the surface is washed, the varnish is removed with alcohol and the lines are retouched with a graver. Thus fashioned the engraving is called line engraving.

To obtain an impression from the plate the incised lines are inked. The surface of the plate is carefully cleaned so that not a spot of ink remains on the parts not incised. The paper is applied to the surface and takes the ink in the lines.

Line engraving is practiced on copper and on steel. The first stamps made at Mauritius, the views of Sydney, the laureated heads of New South Wales and others, permit collectors to understand the system of printing, and to verify its distinctive characteristics. Other stamps, better engraved, have been printed by the same process.

By the use of a second process of engraving the drawing appears in relief. In this case the graver has taken from the plate all the parts of it which did not form a design. Whereas, in the line process the paper on which the drawing is applied, by penetrating into the incised lines to take the ink, presents a relief on the side of the drawing, in the other impression a contrary effect is produced. The printed parts of the relief present an imprint on the recto of the leaf.

In the third process the surfaces which furnish the imprint are quite flat. This is lithography. Everybody knows that Aloys Senefelder invented it. A chalky stone, which is found especially in the neighborhood of Solenhofen, is covered with a drawing made with a special ink or pencil. An application is made on the entire surface of the stone of a solution of acidulated gum with hydro-chloric or nitric acid. The object of the acidulation is to clean the plate and fix the writing or the design, by making the ink or pencil paste insoluble in water. In this way the two substances combined

with that of the stone render the latter insensible to the
action of the oily matter contained in printing ink.   The
roller passes over the entire stone.   The ink adheres
only to the places covered by the drawing or writing,
and water applied to the surface with a sponge prevents
the ink from adhering to other points.   The drawing resulting from this mode of printing has no relief, but gives
to the paper a polished surface.

Here then are the three modes of printing :
1. In line.
2. Typographic.
3. Lithographic.

Nothing seems easier than to recognize at once the different modes of printing, but there are cases when they
are very difficult to verify.

Line engraving is made generally on copper or on steel,
but a lithographic stone also may be engraved.   In such
a case a covering of lampblack and gum and water is
placed on the stone.   The drawing is made through
the covering on the stone by means of a steel or diamond
point.   The ink roll does not stick to the gummed parts
of the stone, but the ink penetrates into the uncovered
parts of it and forms with the stone an insoluble soap.
The surface of the impression is the same, but the first
proofs have the relief impression, which is characteristic
of printing from line engraving.   As an example of that
sort of printing I must cite the two-pence of Victoria, the
first examples of which, brown color, seem as if they
were engraved in line, while the last example, black entirely, do not present this characteristic relief, but a tarn-
ished background, the design having been effaced by long
use of the plate.

Typographic printing is executed either with printing
types or with a plate engraved in relief.   In many cases

an engraving on wood is sufficient.   The finest wood is
selected.   The wood is cut lengthwise.   Copper and
steel are subjected in this process to the same method
as in ordinary line engraving, but when the die is obtained it is multiplied by galvanic process.   The use of
gutta percha has done much for the advancement of this
industry.   Gutta percha is easily managed.   It may be
applied on the object to be reproduced, which will pene-
trate in all the hollows of the model.   When gutta percha
is cold its elasticity permits it being drawn from the mould,
preserving all the fidelity and delicacy of the original.
The mould thus prepared is made a conductor of elec-
tricity by the application of powdered plumbago.   It is
then put into a solution of sulphate of copper.

As examples of engraving in relief on steel, of multiplication of drawings by galvanic process and of typographic impressions of designs thus obtained, one may
refer to the stamps of the French Republic and of the
Empire.

In recent years photo-typography has been used for
French stamps.

This process permits the reduction of details with a
fineness that the most skillful artist could not imitate.
This perfection of work makes counterfeits more and
more difficult, but forgers who know it may reproduce at
small expense ancient and rare stamps.

I shall discuss in another chapter the method of distinguishing the counterfeits.

I do not intend to enter into details of all the different
processes which serve to make plates and to print
stamps.   Collectors may understand the various modes
of printing from what I have said.   I shall only recall
summarily the three kinds of impressions and indicate
briefly the way to distinguish them :

In Line.—The lines of the design come out in relief on the recto of the leaf, and leave on the reverse the traces of a strong pressure.

Typographic.—The design is in relief on the verso of the leaf.   A light gaufering is on the recto of the white part.   There is no appearance of thickness of ink.

Lithographic.—There is no relief of the ink at recto, nor at the verso.   The paper is more or less brilliant.

These are the distinctive characteristics of the three methods of impression: but it is often very difficult to verify them.   How can one, for example, recognize the signs of typographic impression on stamps which have been subjected to cylindrical pressure?   It is only by a daily examination of stamps that collectors can learn to distinguish the different kinds of engraving and of printing.

THE PRINTING OF STAMPS.

There are typographic, engraving and lithographic inks.

The black typographic ink most commonly used is a mixture of oil and flaxseed, to which is added a resinous substance, and lamp black.   It is a sort of greasy varnish. A good printing ink must adhere to the paper without penetrating into it.   It must not form yellow lines around the letters.

The first quality that coloring matter in typographic ink should possess, is that of very fine powder.   Lamp black fills this object perfectly.   To obtain colored powder in the same state, the colors are crushed with a conic instrument known as "molette."   Often the coloring matter has a tendency to disengage itself from the varnish because it is heavy ; at other times, the copper on the galvanic plates reacts on colors and modifies their shades ; but it is useless to dwell on these details which interest a printer more than they do a stamp collector.

THE COLOR OF STAMPS.

Everybody knows that when a ray of solar light is caught in a prism in a dark room it produces on a white background an oblong image called the solar spectrum. Among these colors, one distinguishes six or seven which are simple or elementary.

They are violet, blue, green, yellow and red, for indigo is only a shade of blue. These colors, all coming from a white light, are the result of the unequal refracting qualities of the elementary colors. Of these, red is the one, which deviates the least, while violet is the one which deviates the most. These two colors occupy the two extremities of the spectrum. The reunion of all these colors, through a bi-convex glass, will produce a white light in the focus of the lens. White is therefore the fusion of all colors. Black, on the contrary, is absence of all rays of light.

Among the elementary colors of the spectrum must be distinguished the primitive colors : red, yellow and blue, and the complementary colors, which contain two of the primitive colors that are the complement of a third. Thus green, formed of blue and yellow, is the complement of red ; violet, formed of blue and red, is the complement of yellow ; orange, formed of red and yellow, is the complement of blue. It is useful to recall these details, because they explain how certain colors are obtained by the combination of two primitive colors.

Colors in nature are borrowed from the three kingdoms, animal, vegetable and mineral. The products of these kingdoms furnish the elements which serve for the manufacture of the different colored inks. In general t

colors which come from the vegetable and animal kingdoms are vivid and brilliant, but easily altered in the
light. The colors which are borrowed from the mineral
world are more permanent, although they may be altered
by chemicals.

In the composition of red one finds ordinarily :

Sulphur of mercury or cinnabar, which produces vermilion.

Minium, or peroxide of lead. This substance is easily
altered by sulphurous emanations, and this explains the
black coloration of certain stamps of recent issues.

Oxide of iron, either natural or artificial, which produces
light shades.

Iodide of mercury, a color easily altered.

All these colors are taken from the mineral kingdom.
The following, less solid but more beautiful, come from
the animal and vegetable kingdom.

Cochineal, which comes from an insect, coccus cacty,
of Mexico. By its ebullition in water and the addition of
a small quantity of alum, it furnishes a superb color
called red lacquer and, when the decoction is more con-
centrated, carmine.

Rubia tinctorum, which comes of the root of a plant.

Gum lacquer, a sort of resinous substance taken from a
tree of India.

Dragon blood, a resinous substance found in the fruit
and leaves of an Indian palm tree.

Yellows are formed by :

Chromate of lead, which furnishes chrome yellow and
is easily altered.

A mixture of sulphate and chromate of lead which produces pale colors.

Another mixture of oxides of lead and antimony which
produces Naples yellow. These two colors are easily
altered.

The various silicates of hydrated aluminium.

Sulphate of cadmium, which produces a cadmium yellow, a fixed and brilliant color.

Gutta gum, a resinous substance from a tree of Siam.

Various yellow lacquers obtained from various woods.

Orange is obtained by the combination of red and yellow colors.   Still, there are some natural colors which are not much used, like :

Sulphate of arsenic.

Earth of sienna.

Roucou, which comes of the grains of the Bixa Orellana.

These natural colors are not much used and are probbly never used in stamps.

Blue colors are obtained from :

Lapis lazuli, a Persian stone which produces natural tra marine.   This color, the price of which is high, is replaced by artificial ultra marine.   Chemists say that it is only a silicate of aluminium colored by sulphite of sodium.

Ferrocyanite of iron, which produces Prussian blue, or Paris green.

Several salts of Cobalt that form with aluminium a pink lacquer which turns to blue at red heat.

Indigo, extracted from the Indigo fera tinctoria.

Natural substances do not give much green color. Yet this may be obtained from :

Acetate of copper, or verdigris, which is easily altered.

Malachite, which produces mineral green.

Arsenite of copper, which produces emerald green.

An oxide of chrome green.   In general, manufacturers prefer to mix blues and yellows in order to obtain the various shades of green color.

Purple or violet colors are obtained from :

Garance which produces Garance purple and burnt carmine.

Cochineal, which produces purple lacquer.

Some red ochres.

In fine, ancient purple, is extracted from certain shells.

Several stamps of Afghanistan were printed in this color.

Brown colors are obtained with :

Various silicates of hydrated aluminium, natural or colored by an oxide of manganese and iron which has been designated as earth of Umbra, the name of the Italian city where it is found in a natural state.

A sort of earth which contains an oxide of iron and of manganese and a small quantity of bituminous matter, which forms Vandyck brown.

Asphalt.

Sepia, a natural brown color furnished by the cuttle-fish.

Black is furnished by lampblack.

White is obtained from :

Carbonate of lead.

Carbonate of zinc.

Carbonate of chalk.

There are also gilt inks, or bronze, or silver. Readers whom the question interests should refer to an article in the Philatelic Record, "Notes on Pigments," published in May, 1881.

A great deal of attention has been paid for twenty-five years to coloring matter obtained by chemical process. They are aniline colors, the origin of which deserves mention.

Aniline, obtained at first among the products of the distillation of indigo, then drawn from tar, is obtained artificially now-a-days by the conversion of benzine into nitro-benzine, submitted to the action of such agents as iron and acetic acid. Aniline is a colorless liquid with a specially disagreeable odor.   It is a little denser than water.   It is almost insoluble in water.   It is mingled in all proportions with alcohol, ether and volatile oils.   It possesses the characteristics of an alkaloid.

Certain of its salts mingled with sulphuric acid have produced derivatives used in the preparation of coloring matters the richness and purity of which are incomparable.   The most important of these derivatives is Rosaniline, or fuchsine.

The colors called Hoffman violet, Lyons blue, Paris violet and Aniline green were discovered recently.

DESIGNATION OF COLORS.

If one should read a certain number of stamp catalogues one would soon find that the same colors of stamps are designated by different names ; that the same name serves to indicate diverse colors, and this not only with different authors but through the pages of one book.   On this question there is real anarchy, and every collector who ever tried to make a stamp catalogue, or a list of new stamps, must have regretted the lack of a classification of colors.   The subject has been studied for many years.   I do not pretend to settle it in this chapter.   I propose only to recall the work that has been done.

In 1868, the National Philatelic Society of New York sent to the International Congress at Paris, a request for the creation of a chart of colors.   This demand contained the following plan.

In the first place, take the colors of the prism in their regular order, give to each one its right name in four languages, English, French, German and Italian ; represent each one of the colors by Roman figures, every one of the colors being named and figured, add to it as many samples of shades as may be found necessary, beginning with the lighter shades, and placing them in numerical order. The normal color should occupy the central place and be numbered 4, as in the submitted plan. After the colors of the prism, give the compound colors, like brown, gray, etc., and number them in the same manner.

This demand was accompanied by a specimen of classification in nine columns, comprising :

Roman figures for numbers.

Names of colors.

Seven rectangles to contain the shades of each color.

The advantages which the committee found in this work were that it weighted the memory with only 15 names of colors instead of a hundred and more.

That the shades being numbered uniformly accustom the eye to determining a particular shade through a simple number.

That it made description easier : red, 4, would designate exactly the color and the shade.

This communication gave rise to a report wherein it was demonstrated that it would be impossible to establish at a reasonable price, a chart of fifty colors and shades, An issue of 500 copies only would require 25,000 proofs, even if there were no errors.

Maury thought that it would be better to make a chart with stamps. He showed that the names in catalogues destined to painters and dyers could not serve to name the colors employed in stamps. He made a list of 44 colors or tints, and in the place of these, placed stamps reproducing the colors and tints.

Considering that in every country a small number of houses printed stamps, and that every house constantly made use of the same colors, in small quantity, because the number of values of stamps was limited, Maury decided that by taking successively each country it would be impossible to make a list accompanied with stamps, either new or cancelled reproducing the corresponding colors.

He thought that it would be useless to reunite all the shades, that is all the degrees through which a color may pass without losing its distinguishing name. But he said that it was not thus with tints, that is shades resulting from a mixture of two colors.

The list presented by Maury is interesting, because for each color or tint he quotes one or several stamps with which one may establish a scale of colors.

After the Congress of 1878 had refused to accede to the American demand, the American Society published a pamphlet entitled "A Color Chart." The plates which it contained were made by one of the foremost American printing houses. The work is in 36 pages, divided into four parts. Each one of these reproduces a tint and comprises six shades. The tints are in seven classes, disposed in the following order of colors : Orange, green, blue, purple, brown, slate and red. It is a singular classification. Yellow, a primitive color, is given in it only as a tint of orange.

Moens justly criticised this work, but it should be acknowledged that it has many good traits and deserves to be encouraged. The greatest fault which could be found with it is that in giving the same name to a certain number of tints it fails to distinguish them by other means than numbers to which must be added numbers of shades. This may cause an inextricable confusion. I am not astonished that the American Society have renounced the use of this process to designate colors of stamps. I have thought that it would be possible to make this work profitable by substituting for numbers, names of colors.

But what names? The names which are given to colors used in painting, printing and dyeing are constantly varying. The same color is expressed by a different name in various industries. It seems more rational to me to take the names of colors from those of natural products. It would be easy to verify in every principal country all the shades used in stamps. This would permit the setting aside of a certain number of shades of the Color Chart which were never used. The shades of every tint, reduced to three, might be indicated by the words dark or light for the two extremes.

THE PAPER USED FOR STAMPS.

Formerly the paper was manufactured by hand with metallic frames called forms. A certain quantity of pulp was subjected to a series of operations by which it was compressed, dried and sized. This work is performed nowadays by machinery.

Formerly old rags only were used for paper; nowadays straw, hay, wood and a fibrous grass known in Algeria as alfa, are used. Japan makes use of the blackberry fibre.

Ancient stamp paper and the paper of the first stamps of Cashmere and Japan were hand made. This paper is laid, that is it presents a series of paralled lines reunited by perpendicular lines in wider spaces, which are nothing other than the result of the imprint on the pulp of the metallic threads constituting the form. Nowaday manufacturers have tried to give to machine made paper the same aspect as this ancient paper.

Machine made paper is in various states. At times it is laid; at times it is plain; often it has a fine grain which gives to it an air of mist. At other times it presents an appearance of being studded with sand.   There are no high priced paper vertical and horizontal lines in water-mark.   These are found in certain varities of stamps of Guadalajara and Ecuador.   In Mexico, in the issue of recent years, the paper of stamps is ruled with blue.

Age gives to paper a yellowish tint usually; but there are stamps of a blueish color produced by age.   One finds this color especially in old English stamps.   Bacon print-ed on white paper the one-penny and two-pence stamps, but they have to-day a very pronounced blue color. This effect has been attributed to the action of gum on certain ingredients of the color, but one may find it on proofs which were never gummed.   It may be due to the separation in the paper of one of the coloring matters used in the ink.

Color paper is used to distinguish various stamps and then these are printed in black.   The paper is colored with one of the coloring matters enumerated in the pre-ceding chapter.   It happens to be never colored uni-formly.   White paper is often very thick.   This is of no importance in telegraphic and revenue stamps, the weight of which may increase weight of letters.   Some white paper is glazed; some is as thin as an onion skin.   Much white paper has water-marks which will be the subject of another chapter.   But official water-marks must not be confounded with factory marks.

There are, in some varieties of paper, colored threads which were inserted during the manufacture by a pro-cess called Dickinsons, from the name of its inventor. These varieties have been used for stamps of Bavaria, the second Federal series of Switzerland, the Gothic stamps of Great Britain and in other countries.

Proofs of stamps are printed most often on onion skin paper or China paper.

WATER-MARKS

Water-marks deserve particular attention. I shall write here only of those found on stamp sheets, and refer to a special chapter on envelopes and post-cards for the water-marks which may be found on these. There are two distinct orders of water-marks.

1. The water-mark is composed of a large design the details of which occupy various points of the sheet. The result is that one finds a different part of the design in different parts of the sheet. The first stamps of India are so marked.

In Hungary the sheet is covered with circles that cross one another and bear the letters K. L.

Queensland sheets bear the legend "Queensland Postage Stamps" in capital letters. Sheets of Tuscany bear the ducal crown arranged in horizontal rows, separated by five horizontal lines and one vertical line. These sheets were used for the ducal issues. The sheets of the Government have as water-marks crossed undulations traversed diagonally by a line of inscription H. E. R. R. Poste Toscane.

In the kingdom of the Two Sicilies one finds the fleur-de lis occupying the space of several stamps.

2. The water-mark may be formed not by a large design but by small ones, reproduced on the points that each stamp must occupy. It is understood that the manufacture of stamps is not so carefully done that every one

of them may bear, exactly in the middle of the space that it occupies, the water-mark which was made for it. It happens frequently that one finds in stamps only fragments of their water-marks. Often the water-mark in them is reversed. The fault is not very interesting, because it is very frequent.

Search for these water-marks is often difficult. It is true that one may find them often when the stamps are held to the light, but they are more easily perceived when the stamps are placed on black objects.

The most common water-warks are the following :

1. The Royal Crown. There are the crowns of England, Denmark, India, Italy and Sweden.

2. The Royal Crown of England surmounted by two C C, used specially in the English colonies. The two C's are the initials of Crown Colonies. In the middle of the sheet are the words "Crown Colonies" in water-mark. This water-mark, used from 1863 until 1882, was

replaced in the latter year by the initials C. A., and the crown, meaning Crown Agencies.

3. Oak leaves (Hanover) or laurel (Prussia).

4. The coat of arms of Italy surmounted by the royal crown.

5. Emblems taken from arms of different countries; buckled garter (several types), heraldic flowers, the stem of a rose, a globe surmounted by a cross for Great Britain. An elephant head for India; a pineapple for Jamaica; a lion with an axe for Norway; a swan for Western

Australia; a pyramid surmounted by a rose for Egypt ; a crescent and a star, also for Egypt ; the Tower of Ara-

gon for Spain ; studded forget-me-nots for Lubeck ; an anchor in a triangle for the Cape; an anchor with a cable, a trefoil, a Maltese cross for England ; a sort of shell expressing the Ying and the Yang, that is, all the

oppositions, good and evil, light and darkness, and so on, for China ; the Sankho, another sacred shell, a divine emblem of Vishnu, a wheel for Siam.

6. A post-horn, a well known emblem of the post office for Brunswick, Norway and the Netherlands.

7. Stars with six branches, and with or without points.

8. Lines variously arranged and forming varied designs, as in Spain and Cuba, where there are rows of loops in stamps of 1855, and crossed diagonal lines in stamps of 1856. Stamps of Bavaria have lines forming lozenges or vertical undulations, or loops and ovals.

9. Letters, either capital or interlaced, with or without frame, as in the first issues of Belgium. Letters made of one line, or of a double line, as the W of Luxembourg, or the A of Modena. These letters with single or double line, are often accompanied by the Royal Crown, as in Queensland or Southern Australia.

10. The value of the stamp expressed in English letters, or in antique letters, or in figures made of a single line, and more or less regular, or in figures made of a double line, as in New South Wales.

Observe the singularity of the water-mark which the

syllabic Chinese characters Kong Pou form in one of the last issues of Shanghai.

GUMMING THE STAMPS.

As a stamp is a sign destined to represent the post-office's receipt for duty paid, it is necessary that it should adhere to the letter, and that, by some process of annulling it, it may not be used again.

A certain number of stamps were never gummed. Such were the first stamps of Reunion Island. One finds them bearing the marks of pins, which were used to affix them to letters; or traces of sealing wax. The sender of the letter had the privilege of affixing the stamp as he wished.

The principal substances used are : Gum, dextrine, mucilage. Leroy, in a history of French stamps says, that the operation of gumming necessitates annually the use of 40,000 kilograms of Senegambia gum. The gumming is done by machinery, over which 600 sheets per hour are made to pass.

In England, at first, the adhesive substance used, the "cement on the back" was of a yellowish color, defective in adhesive qualities and very disagreeable to the taste. According to testimony given in 1852 before the House of Commons this substance was composed of potato starch, wheat and gum. The witness added that this starch had been subjected to a slight modification which implied its transformation into dextrine. In 1855

the adhesive matter was strengthened by the addition of
a certain quantity of gelatine.   The color was less dark,
but the taste was as disagreeable as before.   It was ru-
mored, then, that the adhesive substance was a pernicious composition made of fish glue.   The revelation
of the great secret of the British gum taught the public
that the postage stamp "poison" came of potatoes.

PERFORATION OF STAMPS.

When postage stamps were first issued they were
printed in sheets from which they could not be easily detached.   The first English stamps, those of Brazil and of
Zurich and others, before 1854 necessitated the use of
scissors or a knife.   Yet the first attempts to perforate
stamps were made long before that year.

In 1866, when I wrote my first article on this question,
the distinction among the varieties of perforations was
not appreciated in France, and in England it was a subject of sarcasm.   Everybody appreciates to-day the importance of this study.

A perforated stamp is one which bears the trace of a
method of separation from other stamps on a sheet   The
term is generic.   There are two classes of separation :

1.   The division is made in such a way that it leaves
indentations around the frame of the stamp.

2.   The intervals between the stamps were treated
with instruments that separated the fibres of the paper.
The operation is called rouletting.

The words perforated and rouletted have the merit of
being brief and of indicating to collectors at once the
two methods of making the separations.

PERFORATED STAMPS.

Before giving the varieties of perforations and the means of distinguishing them, it may be useful to give the history of the perforating machines originally used.

In 1847 Henry Archer, an Irishman, proposed to the Marquis of Clanricarde, then Postmaster-General, the adoption of a machine which he had invented by means of which stamps could be separated without the use of knife or scissors. The machine was submitted to Bokenham, then director of the circulation department of the post office, and to other administrators, who submitted a report to the Stamp Commissioners, October 14, 1849, recommending the machine as a meritorious and useful invention. In the report of the Stamp Commissioners made to the Lords of the Treasury the invention was described as destined to pierce the folds of the paper between the stamps by a series of small cuts. This system is known to collectors as rouletting. It consists simply in small cuts in the paper without loss of any of its substance. The Lords of the Treasury approved the report.

The first machine offered by Archer consisted of a roulette with thirteen small points destined to cut the stamps in the direction of their width and of another roulette with twenty-one points destined to cut the stamps in the direction of their length.

When a practical trial of the machine was made it was found that the roulettes wore the table on which the sheets were placed, but did not perforate the sheets. Archer modified his machine, but a second trial was not more successful. Samples of stamps resulting from these two experiments are preserved at the post office. Some sheets came into the hands of the public.   In some specimens of stamps from these sheets the sections differ in length, are irregular and seldom square at the angles.   In other specimens the sections are straight and clear cut.

In 1849 Archer, whom Roland Hill aided, offered another machine built with the idea of perforating the intervals between stamps by a series of holes in the substance of the paper.   The first experiments were unsuccessful, but the machine was used after repeated changes. Many of the obstacles in the way of Archer's success were caused by the objections of the stamp contractors.

Specimens of the experiments with Archer's machine present a series of oval, irregular holes.   Many sheets were spoiled, but some were admitted to circulation at the post office.

The principal difficulty was solved by an arrangement of needles so that sixteen holes were pierced in the length of two centimetres.   Archer procured a patent for his machine, and obtained, in 1852, from a committee of the House of Commons a compensation of £4,000.   He paid £2,000 to various machinists who had aided him. He had neither the genius of invention nor the genius of money making.

After Archer's machine had been bought by the Government, James M. Napier received an order to build different machines propelled by steam.   These machines pierced 16 holes in two centimetres, but a change was tried in 1855.   Fourteen holes were placed in the space of sixteen.   It had been found that the steel plates of the machine were easily worn out.   The change was satisfactory.   In 1881 Thomas Peacock constructed machines which pierced 5.500 sheets in an hour.

Perforating machines were used in Sweden in 1855, in the United States in 1856, in Russia and Austria in 1858, in Wurtemburg in 1859, in Baden in 1861, in France and Switzerland in 1862, in Belgium, Italy and Saxony in 1863, in the Netherlands and Hamburg in 1864, and in Spain in 1865.

In France a perforating machine invented by Susse was used in 1861, but official perforation was not adopted until a year later.

Whatever the machine used may be, the result is the production on the separating line of the stamps of small holes which are larger when they are less numerous. Students of perforations in stamps count the number of indentations in one side of the frame, but two stamps of the same sheet may have a difference of one indentation, either as a result of an accident in tearing or of an irregular action of the machine. Two stamps may not have the same number of holes and yet have the same number of indentations.

In order to obtain comparative figures, I propose a unity of conventional length and to count the number of indentations in the length. As the size of postage stamps does not vary much from 23 millemetres, I have proposed two centimetres as a unit which most collectors accept. On a rule where centimetres are figured place the stamp and count the number of holes in the space.

Another system consists in a graded scale which, on a width of two centimetres, gives a series of lines representing each one of the various methods of perforation. At the right of every line is indicated the number of holes to every two centimetres. This dispenses with the trouble of counting them. Westoby made this scale according to my directions and gave to it the name of odontometre which I proposed.

ODOTOMETRE :

Measure of the perforations of stamps.

ODONTOMÈTRE MESURE DE LA PIQURE DES TIMBRES	MODELES DES DIFFÉRENTES VARIÉTÉS DE DENTELURES DES TIMBRES
16	
15 ½	
15	Piqué . . . . ʊʊʊʊʊʊʊʊʊʊʊ
14 ½	
14	Percé en lignes . . . . ------------
13 ½	
13	— en points . . . .
12 ½	
12	—| —| |·. . . . . . . • • • • •
11 ½	— en arc . . . . ᴧᴧᴧᴧᴧᴧᴧᴧ
11	
10 ½	— en scie . . . . ʌʌʌʌʌʌʌʌʌ
10	— en serpentin . . . . ꙮꙮꙮꙮꙮ
9 ½	
9	— — . . . . ꙮꙮꙮꙮꙮ
8 ½	
8	— en pointes . . . . . ʌʌʌʌʌʌ
7 ½	
7	— en losange . . . . . . ∨ ∨ ∨ ∨ ∨ ∨
6 ½	— en trous carrés . . . ⊔ ⊔ ⊔ ⊔ ⊔ ⊔
6	
5 ½	

Examples of the different varieties of indentations in stamps :

> Perforated.
> Rouletted in lines.
>   "   in dots.
>   "   " "
>   "   in arcs.
>   "   in saw teeth.
>   "   in serpentine.
>   "   "
>   "   in points.
>   "   in lozenges.
>   "   in square holes.

ROULETTED STAMPS.

Stamps, the separation of which is facilitated by a simple separation of the fibres of the paper without loss of any of its substance, are said to be rouletted. This is done in seven different ways :

1.   In straight lines, or simply in lines.

2.   In dots, differing from the rouletting in lines only in the form. In the rouletting in dots the latter are square, not like small lines. Examples of it are found in stamps of Mexico, 1872.

3.   In parallel lines. Examples of this may be found in the German 5 and 10 silbergroschen, and 15 and 30 kreuzer.

4.   In arcs. Stamps of Hanover and Brunswick are thus rouletted.

5.   In saw-teeth. Stamps of Bremen are rouletted in this way.

6. In serpentine.

7. In points. This method differs from the preceding one in the triangular form of the indentations. This rouletting is found on certain stamps of the Steamer Robert Todd, for correspondence between St. Thomas and Venezuela.

There is another method of rouletting for which I can find no other name than fanciful. It is found only on revenue stamps of France during the Empire and the beginning of the Republic. It seems as if a separation had been drawn on the sheets with such a roulette as the pastry cooks use. Every stamp, which measures about 47 millemetres in height, presents on each side only two or three indentations, rounded and separated by intervals of similar form reversed.

The various methods of perforating stamps may, like water-marks, be a pretext to seek for certain curious varieties of stamps; this is not the aim of this discussion. I have no other intention than to give to the collector means of distinguishing counterfeit stamps. This is not the time to tell the advantages, other than this, which this study may yield.

SECOND PART.

VARIETIES OF STAMPS.

ELEMENTS OF STAMPS.

Before telling the history of the various stamps, it seems necessary to tell the relative importance of the various elements in the making of a stamp.

Stamps present differences which are due to :

1.   The design.
2.   The legend.
3.   The value and the money.
4.   The plate and the print.
5.   The color.
6.   The nature of the paper.
7.   The presence or absence of water-marks.
8.   The quality of the adhesive substance.
9.   The indentations.

I have explained in what the varieties resulting from these different causes consist. If we examine these elements as a means of classifying the stamps in a collection, we find differences that may:

1.   Be flagrant.
2.   Necessitate a special examination.

The design or type of the stamp is its most important element. A head of the Republic may not be confounded with a head of Napoleon, whether the latter be laureated or not.

The element of the stamp second in importance is the legend. If the substitution of a head of the Republic for that of Napoleon does not permit of confusion between the stamps of 1849-50 with those of 1853, the legend Republic. Franc. and the small B under the collar establishes capital distinction between the stamps of 1852 and those of 1853-54. A series of pence may not be confounded with a series of cents.

Then there is the color. It is the oftenest used test for values when the entire issue is of the same design. It serves also to characterize certain issues. Small values, 1, 2, 4, and 10 of 1876, in France, printed in green, are of the same type and have the same legend as those of 1877, which are in four different colors. The 5, originally green like the others, is the only one which has preserved its color and this has become its own.

Other values have gone through similar changes at different periods. The 1 franc stamp of 1849, called vermilion, is far from being always identical. It was easy to make it pass from vermilion to brown red and carmine red by gradations of tints almost imperceptible. The differences which may be distinguished in the paper, the water-mark, the adhesive substance and the identations, are of lesser value and may only characterize secondary series and varieties.

TERMS USED IN TIMBROLOGY.

ISSUE, SERIES, EDITION.

All the stamps issued by virtue of a special law or of a decree form an issue. Habitually all such stamps are placed in circulation the same day, either because their introduction is a novelty or because their predecessors have been demonetized; but this is far from being the case always. If certain values of a series are still held in great number, or if the new ones are not yet ready in their entirety, the circulation of the new corresponding values may be long delayed. It is not, therefore, by the first day of their circulation, but by the date of the decree ordering them, that issues are to be designated.

But the word issue has not been applied only to an issue of stamps having common characteristics of the first order. When one studies them, one observes that there are among them series or groups having a secondary characteristic in common, as a water mark, specially distinguishing them. Thus at Hong Kong the stamps of 1862 are on plain paper. The stamps of 1863 have the

water mark C. C. and the crown.   Are these an issue or
a simple series?   The difference, without being as salient
as that of a type or of a color, is not so subtle as to require great attention to be recognized; but should the
amateur having a restricted collection make the distinc-,
tion?   Stamps of one issue should undergo various
changes in details of manufacture, and the public may
never be warned of them.   The first day of the circulation of stamps is hardly ever known accurately.   As the
value of a water mark is only of a secondary order, I
should think that the Hong Kong stamp of 1863 should
be only a series, or better, an edition, and not an issue.
Others would call it an issue.   They and I note the
date.

An issue was characterized : 1, by the law or the decree ordering it; 2, by the legend; 3, by the mode of
printing; 4, by the change in colors; 5, by the change
in money.   There should be noted the frequent issues of
temporary series, characterized by the use on ancient
stamps of a surcharge of new money values.

An edition consists of the values placed in circulation
at one epoch, presenting characteristics of the first order,
and others of lesser importance.   My idea is that the
word edition should be applied to the varieties due to
printing on a special kind of paper, and that series should
express the entire number of stamps of an issue or of an
edition.

TYPE IN STAMPS.

The word type is applied to every subject represented
on a stamp.   For example : Type, portrait of Queen Victoria; type, Britannia; type, head of the French republic.
In other words, type is synonymous with design.   It

may happen that all the parts of the design are not absolutely similar. Thus the present series of English stamps has a profile portrait of Queen Victoria, the size of which is not always identical, and the frame of which varies with the value of the different stamps. It is enough that the central part should be identical. The type is the same in all the stamps; there are only differences of frame, and these differences are not great enough to be designated as types.

If one examines attentively the idea of a stamp one may find slight modifications in it, indicating that from time to time the design has been retouched. For example, the head of the Republic engraved in France in 1849 presents the same general design, the same type, as the same head reproduced on the stamps issued at Bordeaux, but the latter differ in small things, visible only through a magnifying glass. It is for such differences that I have proposed the word " sub-type," which means a small difference in drawing.

VARIETY IN STAMPS.

Variety in stamps is a distinction of secondary order. The stamps are of the same type, but have :

Differences in design.

Differences in color, resulting from degrees in shades or tints.

Differences in paper.

Differences in water-marks.

Differences in gum.

Differences in indentation, perforation, rouletting of all sorts.

In post cards there are differences resulting from the

size of the card, the design and composition, the color and the print.   All these varieties should not be confounded under the name of types.   Since the name of type designates the design, why should it be used for varieties of a different order?

It is understood that single and double post cards are not types.   The varieties which they may offer are types only by the dispositions of their legends, or the nature of the letters entering into their composition.   There must be a difference in the design to constitute a type or a subtype.

ERRORS OR FAULTS IN STAMPS.

Faults in stamps are deviations from custom in stamp making.

There are errors of color, printing, paper, water-mark and value.

Errors in color may be easily confounded with proofs. Proofs may be made on the paper which has been adopted for the manufacture of the stamps, but in general they are not perforated.   Their color is more vivid and more brilliant.   Their edition is better, for it is made with care, from new dies or plates in a small quantity.   Proofs are taken of single stamps and their reverse, usually, is not gummed.

Errors in color occur, often separately, on sheets, the value of which is different.   For example, the 15 centimes of France with picture of the Republic, is printed in red on pink, on a sheet of 10 centime stamps.

In Roumania the 5 bani blue has been printed on a sheet of the 10 bani of 1876.   When such faults are found one should preserve them with one or two stamps at least of the ordinary sheet.   Faults on an entire sheet must be excessively scarce.

There are errors of paper and water-mark.   In New South Wales the 2 was used for the 3, the 8 for the 6 or the 12. A sheet of one paper was used instead of another. When the water-mark is found reversed, certain collectors call it a fault, but the fault is too common to be interesting.

Among errors are faults of print resulting from the breaking of a letter, or its erasure when the plate was worn ; errors of engraving resulting from omission of a letter, as in the plate of the Real blue of the Phillipine Islands, whereof a stamp bears Corros instead of Correos. It is well to preserve by the side of the eroneous stamp one or two ordinary stamps.

This leads me to note a sort of error which is called in France "tete-beche." The word is used to designate two stamps, one of which is printed upside down. The accident results from the reversing of one of the blocks used in printing the sheets. There are cases when the central parts of stamps were reversed while the frame retained its normal position. As an example may be quoted the 12 cuartos of Spain, 1865. The stamp is printed in two colors, blue for the frame, and pink for the portrait, and necessitated the use of two separate blocks. The central part alone was reversed.

It has been said that the presence of a " tete-beche " in a sheet indicates a secret mark of the printing office. The object of it would be to verify counterfeits, but it seems to me to be a singular idea that counterfeits may be verified in sheets.

MOVABLE POSTAGE STAMPS.

The first postage stamps issued were movable stamps. The 1 penny black and 2 pence blue of Great Britain are the first specimens. The first specimens of stamped envelopes are the Mulready envelopes.

In the following years movable stamps were adopted preferably.

The right and left of the postage stamps are not designated in timbrology as in heraldry. In heraldry the shield being considered as carried by its owner has its right at his right. In stamps, the left and right are at the left and right of the person who faces them. This difference may be the source of capital errors. I have often thought that stamps have so many relations with blazonry that the words right and left should mean the same thing in both. My proposition to do this has not been accepted and it is still usage to name the sides of a stamp after the sides of the person who faces it.

This study of movable postage stamps is to be finished with a list of all the countries that have issued them in chronological order. All the issues have not the same value. First come those of all the sovereign states and their principal possessions. I have placed in the list some private post offices which I have indicated by the letters P. O. It often happens that a country making use of a series common to other countries has had to practice surcharges in order to replace lacking values. These surcharged stamps are in use only in that country. I have indicated them by the letters S. I. S., meaning special issue by surcharge. Other countries had an issue of their own and suppressed it in order to use the general series prepared by a new government. The letter O at the end of a line indicates the suppression of stamps after annexation or fusion with a neighboring country.

CHRONOLOGICAL LIST OF COUNTRIES THAT HAVE ISSUED MOVABLE STAMPS.

1, Great Britain, May 6. 1840; 2, Zurich, March 1, 1843. O; 3, Brazil, July 1, 1843: 4, Geneva, Sept. 30, 1843,

O; 5, Basle, July 1, 1845, O; 6, Trinidad, P. O., April 16, 1847, O; 7, United States of America, July 1, 1847; 8. Mauritius, October, 1847; 9, France, January 1, 1849; 10. Belgium, July 1, 1849; 11, Bavaria, November 1, 1849; 12, Spain, January 1, 1850; 13, New South Wales, January 1, 1850; 14, Victoria, January 1, 1850; 15, Switzerland, April 5, 1850; 16, Austria, June 1, 1850; 17, Lombardo-Venetia, June 1, 1850, O; 18, English Guiana, July 1, 1850; 19, Saxony, July 1, 1850, O; 20, Prussia, November 15, 1850, O; 21, Schleswig-Holstein, November 15, 1850, O; 22, Hanover, December 1, 1850, O; 23, Scinde, 1850; 24, Sardinia, January 1, 1851; 25, Denmark, April 1, 1851; 26, Tuscany, April 1, 1851, O; 27, Trinity, April 11, 1851; 28, Canada, April 21, 1851, O; 29, Baden, May 1, 1851, O. 30, New Brunswick, September 6, 1851, O, 31, Nova Scotia, September 1, 1851, O; 32, Hawaii, October 1, 1851; 33, Wurtemburg, October 15, 1851; 34, Brunswick, January 1, 1852, O; 35, Papal States, January 1, 1853, O; 36, Netherlands, January 1, 1852; 37, Reunion Islands, January 1, 1852, O; 38, Office Tour-and-Taxis, P. O., January 1, 1852, O; 39, Oldenburg, January 5, 1852, O; 40, Barbadoes, April 17, 1852; 41, Parma, June 1, 1852; 42, Modena, September 4, 1852, O; 43, Luxembourg, September 15, 1852; 44, Chili, October 20, 1852; 45, Cape Good Hope, January 3, 1853; 46, Portugal, July 1, 1853; 47, Tasmania, November 1, 1853; 48, Phillipine Islands, February 1, 1854; 49, English Indies, May 1854; 50 Norway, September 29, 1854; 51, Western Australia, end of 1854; 52, Ceylon, end of 1854; 53, Spanish West Indies, January 1, 1855; 54, South Australia, January 1, 1855; 55, Bremen. April 10, 1855; 56, Sweden, July 1, 1855; 57, New Zealand, July 13, 1855; 58, Danish West Indies, Nov. 1, 1855; 59, Finland, February 12, 1856; 60, Corrientes, February 29, 1856, O; 61, Mecklemburg-Schwerin, July 1,

1856, O ; 62, Mexico, July 15, 1856 ; 63, Uruguay, October, 1856 ; 64, Saint Helena, 1856 ; 65, Newfoundland, January, 1857 ; 66, Natal, June 1, 1857 ; 67, Peru, December 1, 1857 ; 68, Russia, December 10, 1857 ; 69, Naples, January 1, 1858, O ; 70, New Caledonia, January 1, 1858, O ; 71, Pacific Ocean Company, P. O., March, 1858, O ; 72, Buenos Ayres, April 29, 1858, O ; 73, Argentine Republic, May 1, 1858 ; 74, Moldavia, July 15, 1858, O ; 75, Cordova, end of 1858, O ; 76, Hamburg, January 1, 1859, O ; 77, Lubeck, January 1, 1859, O ; 78, Sicily, January 1, 1859 ; 79, Venzuela, January 1, 1859 ; 80, New Grenada, Colombia, May 1, 1859 ; 81, Ionian Islands, May 15, 1859, O ; 82, Bahamas, June 10, 1859 ; 83, French Colonies, July 1, 1859 ; 84, Romagna, September 18, 1859, O ; 85, Poland, January 1, 1860, O ; 86, Jamaica, November 23, 1860 ; 87, Queensland, November 11, 1860; 88, Malta, December 1. 1860 ; 89, Santa-Lucia, December 15, 1860 ; 90, Prince Edward Island, January 1, 1861, O ; 91, Neopolitan Provinces of Italy, April 1, 1861, O ; 92, Saint Vincent, May, 1861 ; 93, Grenada Island, June 1, 1861 ; 94, Greece, 1–13, 1861 ; 95. Bergedorf, November 1, 1861, O ; 96, Liberia, November 1, 1861, O ; 97, Columbia and Vancouver, 1861, O ; 98, Confederate States of America, 1861, O ; 99, Nevis. 1861 ; 100, Sierra Leone, 1861 ; 101, Italy, March 1, 1862 ; 102, Roumania, June 25, 1862 ; 103, Hong Kong, October, 1862 ; 104, Nicaragua, December 2, 1862 ; 105, Costa Rica, December 2, 1862 ; 106, Antigua, 1862 ; 107, Livonia, 1862, O ; 108, Cuernavaca, 1862, O : 109, Turkey, January 1, 1863 ; 110, Bolivar, February, 1863 ; 111, Russian Levant Co., P. O., January, 1864 ; 112, Holstein and Lauenburg, March 1. 1864, O ; 113, Schleswig, March 15, 1864, O ; 114, Dutch Indies, February 1, 1864; 115, Office Robert Todd, P. O.,

July, 1864, O; 116, Mecklemburg-Strelitz, October 1, 1864, O; 117, Soruth 1864; 118, Ecuador, January 1, 1865, O; 119, Vancouver, July 1, 1865, O; 120, Bermuda, September 13, 1865; 121, Jumoo, September, 1865, O; 122, Cashmere, September, 1865, O; 123, Shanghai, October, 1865; 124, British Columbia, November 1, 1865; 125, Egypt, January 1, 1866; 126, British Honduras, January 1, 1866; 127, Honduras (Republic), January 1, 1866; 128, Company of the Danube P. O., August 1, 1866, O; 129, Servia, October 1, 1866; 130, Virgin Islands, December, 1866; 131, Gambia, 1866; 132, Hyderabad, 1866; 133, Heligoland, January 1, 1867, O; 134, Islands of Turk, April 4, 1867; 135, Queretaro, May 15, 1867; 136, Austrian Levant, June 1, 1867; 137, Bolivia, July 1, 1867; 138, Straits' Settlements, September, 1867; 139, Guadalajara, 1867, O; 140, Chiapas, 1867, O; 141, Monterey, 1867, O; 142, Campeche, 1867, O; 143, Morelia, 1867, O; 144, Oaxaca, 1867, O; 145, Zacatecas, 1867, O; 146, Salvador, 1867; 147, Azores, January 1, 1868; 148, Germany (North Confederation), January 1, 1868, O; 149, Madeira, January 1, 1868, O; 150, Orange, January 1, 1868; 151, Dominion of Canada, March, 1868; 152, Fernando, P. O., July 1, 1868; 153, Suez Company, P. O., July 1, 1868, O; 154, Antioch, 1868; 155, Persia, 1868; 156, Savawak, May 1, 1869; 157, Transvaal, September, 1869; 158, Saint Thomas and Prince, December 14, 1869; 159, Saint Christopher, April 1, 1870; 160, Angola, July 1, 1870; 161, Cundinamarca, July, 1870; 162, Paraguay, August 1, 1870; 163, Alsace-Lorraine, September 6, 1870, O; 164, Afghanistan, 1870; 165, Tolima, 1870; 166, Guatemala, January 1871; 167, Japan, April, 1871; 168, Hungary, May 1, 1871; 169, Portuguese Indies, September 1, 1871; 170, German Empire, December 15, 1871; 171, Fi ji, end of 1871; 172, Iceland, January 1, 1873; 173, Curacoa, June 1, 1873; 174, Porto

Rico, June 1, 1873; 175, Dutch Guiana, October 1, 1873;
176, Italian Levant, January 1, 1874; 177, Domingo,
May 4, 1874 ; 178, Montenegro, May, 1874 ; 179,
Griqualand, end of 1874; 180, Lagos, end of 1874;
181, Gold Coast, end of 1875; 182, Jhind, end of 1875;
183, Montserrat, September, 1876; 184, Cape Verd, January 1, 1877: 185, Cuba, January 1, 1877; 186, Mozambique, March 1, 1877; 187, Nowanaggar, July, 1877; 188,
Samoa, July, 1877; 189, Saint-Marin, August 1, 1877;
190, Alwar, 1877; 191, Bhopal, 1877 ; 192, Faridkot,
1877; 193, Jummoo, Cashmere, June, 1878; 194, Falk-
land, June 19, 1878; 195, Ports of China, August, 1878;
196, Panama, January, 1879; 197, Simoor, January, 1879 ;
198, Bulgaria, May 1, 1879 ; 199, Labouan, May, 1879;
200, Bosnia-Herzegovina, July, 1879; 201, Tobago, Aug.
1, 1879; 202, Bhore, 1879; 203, Cyprus, April, 1880;
204, Rajpecpla, June 1, 1880; 205, Bikanir, 1880; 206,
Perak, 1880; 207, Sunjey Uj ng, :880; 208, East Roumelia, January 19, 1881; 209, Portuguese Guinea, January, 1881; 210, Hayti, July, 1881; 211, Nepal, end
of 188:; 212, Tahiti, end of 1882; 213, Consulate of
Bankok, end of 1882; 214, Selangor, end of 1882; 215,
North of Borneo, May, 1883; 216, Siam, July 16, 1883;
217, Timor, 1883; 218, Stellaland, January, 1884; 219,
Guadeloupe, March 1, 1884; 220, Consulate of Madagascar,
P. O., March, 1884, O; 221, Macao, March, 1884; 222,
German Levant, April 1, 1884; 223, Santander, June,
1884; 224, Puttiala, October 1, 1884; 225, Corea, November 1, 1884, O; 226, Pountch, end of 1884; 227, Saint-
Pierre and Miquelon, S. I. S., January 6, 1885; 228, English Levant, April 1, 1885; 229, Monaco, July 1, 1885;
230, Nabha, July 1, 1885; 231, Gwalier, July 1, 1885;
232, Johore, July 1, 1885; 233, French Levant, August
16, 1885; 234, South Bulgaria, September 22, 1885, O;

235, Guanacaste, November, 1885; 236, Gibraltar, January 1, 1886; 237 British Bechuanaland, January 1, 1886; 238, Holkar, January 1, 1886; 239, New Republic South Africa, January 1. 1886; 240, Cochin-China, S. I. S., May 16, 1886; 241, Martinique, S. I. S., July, 1886; 242, Gabon-Congo, S. I. S., August 1, 1885; 243, Chamba, August, 1886; 244, Tonga, September, 1886; 245, French Guina, S. I. S., December, 1886; 246, Bok hara. P. O., 1886, O; 247, Senegal, April 8, 1887; 248, Jhalawar, July, 1887; 249, Annam and Tonkin, S. I. S., Jan. 21, 1888; 250, Zululand, Jan. 21, 1888; 251, Tunis, July 1, 1888; 252, British Protectorate, July 28, 1888; 253, Wadhwan, end of 1888; 254, Travancore, end of 1888; 255, Formosa, end of 1888; 256, Indo-China, S.I.S., Jan. 8, 1889; 257, Madagascar, S.I.S., March 1889; 258, Nossi-Be, S. I. S., June 4, 1889; 259, Swazieland, Oct. 8, 1889; 260, Pahang, end of 1889; 261, Diego-Suarez, S. I. S., Jan. 25, 1890; 262, Bamra, January 1890; 263, Seychelles. April 5, 1890; 264, Central Africa, July 1890; 265, Leeward Islands, October 31, 1890; 266; Eastern Africa, end of 1890; 267, Tangier, (French bureau), January 1, 1891; 268, Nandgham, January 1, 1891; 269, Terra del Fuego, January 1, 1891; 270, Negri Sembilan, July 1891; 271, Morocco, P. O., 1891; 272, Obock, S. I. S., January 1894; 273, Benin, August 16, 1892; 274, Ivory Coast, end of 1892; 275, French Guinea, end of 1892; 276, French Indies, end of 1892; 277, Mayotte, end of 1892; 278, Oceania, end of 1892; 279, Sultana of Anjouan, end of 1892; 280, Cochin, end of 1892; 281, Cook Islands, end of 1892; 282, Erythrea, February 1, 1893; 283, German East Africa, 1893; 284, Hankow, 1893; 285, Chefoo, 1893; 286, Protectorate of the Niger Coast, 1893.

STAMPED ENVELOPES.

The use of stamped envelopes is as ancient as that of
movable stamps. The Mulready envelopes have in England the same date as the movable stamps; in Finland,
stamped envelopes preceded in 1845 movable stamps,
but if some countries like Prussia and Germany followed
the example of Great Britain, elsewhere envelopes were
adopted only a great deal later. In France they were
not issued before 1882.

Other countries have never used them.

In the study of stamped envelopes the stamp and the
envelope must be considered separately. The stamps
have most of the peculiarities noted in movable stamps.
In form they are square, round, oval, hexagonal, octagonal or irregular. The size is as varied. At first the
size was larger than that of the movable stamps of the
first issues. In some cases, as in the Mulready case, the
design covers the envelope.

What I have said of the frame and the central part of
movable stamps is applicable to the stamps of stamped
envelopes. By the portraits, allegorical figures or coats-
of-arms one may determine the country that issued them,
but the legend completes the information. The legend
gives names of countries, indications relative to the use
of the stamps, value in figures, and in letters, names of
moneys. These details have been recalled about
movable stamps.

The manufacture of blocks and the printing of stamps
are effected by the same processes: line engraving, engraving in relief, lithography. It must be observed that
a part of the stamp is often gaufered in white on color,

a gaufering which makes the design of the central part stand out.

A few words will suffice to explain this method of printing. The dies used in the manufacture of stamped envelopes in relief are prepared by the same method as those incised. For example if a portrait is to be engraved, a large and profound incision is made for the head; other incisions reproduce all the details of figure and diadem. An oval frame, for example, presents wavy and interlaced lines, partly traversed by the letters of the legend. which are on a level with the surface of the die. The die is inked like the typographic plates.

The colors used are the same as those of the movable stamps.

The paper on which the stamps are printed is that of the envelope. The place of the stamp on the envelope varies. On the oldest envelopes the stamp appears at the upper left corner. Experience taught that it was better to place the stamp on the right. On certain envelopes, as the first of Russia, the stamp is placed on the flap.

Stamped envelopes are either official or private. In France and other countries anybody may send envelopes to the post office to be stamped under restrictions of size only.

Envelopes are large, small, medium or oblong, but they vary infinitely in size. Whereas in England the largest envelopes measure 123 by 87 millemetres and the smallest measure 101 by 64 millemetres, in Prussia and in Germany all stamped envelopes are of two sizes, 148 by 115 millemetres, and 148 by 85 millemetres. In the United States sizes vary from 258 to 110 (extra official); 117 to 91 (small baronial); and 135 to 73 (small note). Every intermediate variety has a name, which does not always indicate the same size, being a special name of its manufacturer. One of the largest envelopes is the 50-centavos of Peru, measuring 225 by 180 millemetres.

If one open and entirely undo envelopes on a table one may verify that the four flaps superior, inferior and lateral, are far from being identical in form. The form depends entirely on the manufacturer who supplies the envelopes. American collectors have attached great importance to distinctions of form in envelopes. There is a long list of them in Horner's work, "History and Catalogue of the Stamped Envelopes of the United States."

Japan has a certain variety of long envelopes in the form of bags closed at one extremity by a rectangular flap.

The first English envelopes, called Mulready, had two forms : The envelope, properly so called, and the cover which one folded. Such covers have been in use in countries like Germany, but they reached a higher stage of perfection in the Indies, where the two ends intersect each other and may be sealed. The coloring of the paper varies. It may be white, straw, salmon, azure, manilla, olive, yellow, fawn or orange. Orange has been specially used in the United States in wrappers. White is the most common official color. Envelopes in the United States are of an infinite variety of paper. There are envelopes the interior of which is colored. The object of this is probably to prevent the reading of letters through the paper of the envelope.

All the varieties of paper may be plain. Most ordinarily they are laid and have a water-mark, which is the mark of the manufacturer. But they may have real water-marks covering the envelope as does the fortress of Hamburg or the eagle of Russia. The latter was originally in an oval, but appeared later in a rectangle. A round shield with arms of Mexico appears in Mexico's envelopes of 1884. Bavarian envelopes have wavy lines. Egyptian envelopes are inscribed in water-mark, "Postes Egyptiennes." United States water-marks vary according to issues. In the first, the letters P. O. D. U. S. in two lines and in oblique rows appear. In September, 1870, envelopes printed by G. H. Reay, in New York, appeared with a new water-mark. This consisted of the same five letters interlaced. In 1876 a special water-mark was made for the centennial of the Declaration of Independence. It consisted of a large U containing an S traversed by an oblong C (United States Centennial). Among the lines were four figures forming the year 1876.

In 1879 the water-mark P. O. D. U. S. reappeared in a monogram, but with a star at the intersection of two diagonal lines uniting four of the monograms. In 1883 the star was replaced by the figures 82. In 1886 the monogram U. S. was adopted. The S enlaced the two lines of the U. In 1890 it enlaced only one of the U lines. Then there were special envelopes for the post office, wherein the two letters U. S. are traversed by an oblong band bearing the inscription Postal Service.

Some Swiss envelopes have the water-mark of a dove carrying a letter (1867), and others a shield with a federal cross in the middle of a square, the four corners of which have the figures 10, representing the value of the envelope (1875). In 1874 appeared 5-centime envelopes bearing a large figure 5 in double lines in water-mark. A fourth variety of envelopes bears in water-mark an oblique band with the Federal shield in arabesques (1879).

Denmark and the Danish Indies have envelopes, the flap of which is ornamented with a royal crown in water-

mark.   In Austria, since 1865, letters in double lines form
the word, Brief-Couverts in various types.

The greater number of envelopes have no gaufered seal
on the flap, and some official envelopes have.   The first
stamped envelopes of the German States, Prussia, Mecklemberg-Schwerin, have an oval design measuring 19
millemetres by 15.   Prussia used two round seals, one

A   B   C

measuring 18 millemetres (B), the other 16 millemetres
(C).   In one of the editions of 1858, a seal was used, the
central part of which was a star with six points (D).   Later a rose was used (E).   The office of Tour and Taxis

D   E   F

used a post horn, of which there are two varieties, differing only in size.   The various states of Germany, Baden,
Brunswick, Mecklemberg-Schwerin, Strelitz and Oldenberg, the envelopes of which were doubtless made in
Berlin, were water-marked with these various designs according to the time of issue and edition.   Saxony had at
first a special design in interlaced curved lines, and later a
fleuron.   Hanover had a seal of 18 millemetres, the centre of which was a post horn.   The Confederation of
Northern Germany and the Empire continued the use of
these various seals.   Wurtemburg uses a large rose measuring 18 millemetres with big dots in two concentric cir-

cles in the middle; another rose, almost similar, with five
circles instead of two; a post horn with figures of value

G   H   I

in the centre, and the Kingdom's coat of arms between
two oak branches in a circle. Bavaria uses two roses
with post horn in the middle, and a seal of the Kingdom similar to that of Wurtemburg.

J   K   L

Austria-Hungary has several types of roses. Switzerland has a special rose design. England has two varieties of heraldic flowers. At first, Ceylon and Mauritius
had two fantastic seals which served to disinguish the
time of issue. India has an elephant under a palm tree.

M   N   O

Uruguay, a rising sun on waves, Victoria, New South
Wales and Hyderabad have a certain number of seals of
interlaced lines in a garter, which do not appear to be
official

The gum on the flap of envelopes may give useful indication for the classification of simple varieties resulting
from editions. For example, the first envelopes of the

German States have at the point of the flap only two centimetres of gum.   It was the result of a single stroke of

P   Q   R

the brush on a certain number of envelopes placed
upon one another in advance.   Later the gum was applied on a greater width of envelopes, and nowadays it
covers the edge of the entire length of the flap.

The first Mulready envelopes and wrappers were traversed by silk threads.   These threads appear on the first
envelopes with gaufered portrait.   They cut obliquely the
corner where the gaufered stamp is.   Prussian envelopes
of the first series have the same threads, but these were
replaced by two oblique lines printed in diamond type
composed of the words "Post Couvert."   The color of
these lines varies.   The color is gray or black in Prussia,
and violet in the first issue of Tour and Taxis.   These inscriptions were suppressed in 1872.

The number of values of stamps printed on official envelopes has varied in every country and according to
epochs.   In England envelopes of the first issues were
of 1 penny and 2 pence.   The 2½ pence envelopes were
not issued until 1892.   In Prussia the first issue had the
number 7, but this was reduced later to 4, and later to 3.
In France there are only two values, 5 centimes for vis-
iting cards and circulars and 15 centimes for letters.

Individuals have taken advantage of the privilege to
print all sorts of values on all sorts of paper for stamped
envelopes.   In England there are envelopes with two
stamps the value of which has no relation to the usual
post duties.   Such envelopes are not really worthy of

interest. There are also envelopes with names of firms addressed, but it seems to me that their collection is very superfluous.

Registered envelopes issued in England and in a certain number of its colonies, are manufactured of paper lined with linen to prevent their tearing. Their sizes are as follows:

293	by 153	millemetres.
252	" 175	"
225	" 100	"
200	" 126	"
150	" 98	"
132	" 82	"

They have the form of the Japanese envelopes called bags, that are closed at one of the ends. On the flap is applied the registry stamp which is gaufered. The face of the envelope contains various instructions, the word Registered and an R in an oval. Two straight lines printed in blue or in red like the instructions, one lengthwise and the other crosswise, meet on the two sides of the envelope. This is to simulate the green tape which formerly tied, in England, letters containing money. It is on the face of the envelope where the instructions are printed that the movable stamps are affixed.

These registered envelopes are so useful that I should ike to see them adopted in France.

CHRONOLOGICAL LIST OF THE COUNTRIES WHICH HAVE ISSUED STAMPED ENVELOPES.

1, Great Britain, May 5, 1840; 2, Finland, January, 1, 1845; 3, Geneva, February, 1846, O; 4, Russia, December 1, 1848; 5, Hanover, May 15, 1849,O; 6, Prussia, September 15, 1851, O; 7, United States, August 4, 1853; 8, Brunswick, August 1, 1855, O; 9, Mecklemberg-Schwerin, July 1, 1856, O; 10, Bremen, January 1857, O; 11, English Indies, 1857; 12, Baden, October, 1858, O; 13, Ceylon, October, 1858; 14, Saxony, July 1, 1859 O; 15, Poland, January, 1860, O; 16, Canada, February 1, 1860; 17, Oldenberg, December 15, 1860, O; 18, Austria, January 1, 1861; 19, Lombardo-Venetia, January 1, 1861, O; 20, Office Tour and Taxis, P. O., October 1, 1861, O; 21, Mauritius, December 1861; 22, Wurtemberg, Oct. 1, 1862; 23, Lubeck, July 1, 1863, O; 24, Mecklemberg-Schwerin, October 1, 1864, O; 25, Denmark, Jan. 1865; 26, Hamburg, April 5, 1866, O; 27, Uruguay, April, 1866; 28, Austria Levant, June, 1867; 30, Brazil, July, 1867; 31, Germany (North Confederation), December, 1868, O; 32, Bavaria, February 1, 1869; 33, Transvaal, March, 1869; 34, Vicoria, November 1, 1869; 35, Turkey, January 1, 1870; 36, New South Wales, January 1, 1870; 37, Hungary, May 1, 1871; 38, German Empire, December, 1871; 39, Norway, January 1, 1872; 40, Sweden, January 1, 1872; 41, Chili, November 21, 1872; 42, Belgium, August 1, 1873; 43, Japan, December 1873; 44, Mexico, May 5, 1874; 45, Peru, January 1, 1875; 46, Heligoland, January 1, 1875, O; 47, Guatemala, April, 1875; 48, Rajapeepla, 1875; 49, Netherlands, January 1, 1876; 50, Argentine Republic, August 1, 1876; 51, Danish West Indies, September 27, 1877; 52, Persia, 1877; 53, Dutch Indies, January 1, 1878; 54, Hyderabad, January 1, 1878; 55, Portugal, January 1, 1879; 56, Azores, January 1, 1879; 57, Madeira, January, 1879; 58, Queensland, 1880; 59, Bahamas, March, 1881; 60, Republic of San Domingo, September, 1881; 61, Bosnia-Herzegovina, January, 1882; 62, France, October 1, 1882; 63, Barbadoes, October 5, 1882; 64, Tasmania, April 2, 1883; 65, Hawaii, June, 1884; 66, Puttiala, October

1, 1884; 67, Gwalior, July 1, 1885; 68, Jhind, July 1, 1885; 69, Nabha, July 1, 1885; 70, Monaco, April 1, 1886; 71, Costa-Rica, June 15, 1886; 72, Chamba, August, 1886; 73, Egypt, January 1, 1887; 74, Faridkot, January, 1887; 75, South African Republic, January, 1887; 76, Paraguay, March, 1887; 77, Bolivia, May, 1887; 78, Ecuador, July, 1887; 79, Salvador, July, 1887; 80, Tunis, July 1, 1888; 81, Nicaragua, 1888; 82, French Colonies, January, 1889; 83, German Levant, December, 1889; 84, Newfoundland, 1889; 85, Bamra, January 1; 1890; 86, Republic of Honduras, January 1, 1890; 87, Colombia, end of 1890; 88, Liberia, end of 1890; 89, Travancore, 1890; 90, Leeward Islands, June, 1891; 91, Tonga, January 1, 1892; 92, Cochin, April 1, 1892; 93, Cape of Good Hope, June, 1892; 94, Queensland, 1892; 95, Sultana of Anjouan, January, 1893; 96, French Congo, January, 1893; 97, Ivory Coast, January, 1893; 98, Diego-Suarez, January, 1893; 99, Guadeloupe, January, 1893; 100, French Guinea, January, 1893; 101, French GUIANA; 102, French Indes, January, 1893; 103, Indo-China, January, 1893; 104, Martinique January, 1893; 105, Mayotte, January, 1893; 106, New Caledonia, January, 1893; 107, Obock, January, 1893; 108, Oceanica, January, 1893; 109, Reunion, January, 1893; 110, Saint Pierre and Miquelon, January, 1893; 111, Senegal, January, 1893; 112 Benin, January, 1893; 113, English Levant, April 20, 1893.

ENVELOPES REGISTERED.

1, Hungary, April 1, 1874; 2, Austria, end of 1876; 3, Great Britain, January 1, 1878; 4, Bosnia-Herzegovina, 1879; 5, Ceylon, January 1, 1880; 6, New South Wales, March 6, 1880; 7, Cyprus, April, 1880; 8, Trinity, 1880; 9, Queensland, 1880; 10, Jamaica, January 1, 1881; 11, English Guiana, March 24, 1881; 12, Victoria, June, 1881;

13, Colombia, 1881; 14, Turk Islands, 1881; 15, Barbadoes, October 5, 1882; 16, Liberia, July, 1882; 17, Cape of Good Hope, October, 1882; 18, Tasmania, April 2, 1883; 19, Malta, January, 1885; 20, English Indies, May 1, 1886; 21, Gibraltar, January 1, 1886; 22, Grenada, June, 1886; 23, Bechuanaland, July, 1886; 24, New Zealand, October, 1886; 25, Santa-Lucia, December 20, 1887; 26, Chamba, end of 1888; 27, Gold Coast, end of 1888; 28, British Protectorate, end of 1888; 29, Faridkot, July, 1889; 30, Puttiala, July, 1889; 31, Nabha, end of 1890; 32, Malacca, January, 1891; 33, Mauritius, February 6, 1891; 34, Leeward Islands, June 1, 1891; 35, Tonga, October 1, 1891; 36, Gwalior, end of 1891; 37, Eastern Africa, March, 1891; 38, Bermuda, March, 1892; 39, Tobago, end of 1892; 40, South Africa, end of 1892; 41, Oil Rivers, end of 1892.

STAMPED WRAPPERS.

The use of stamped wrappers is not as extended as that of envelopes. If one consult the chronological list which I have made, one may find that the first stamped wrapper was issued by the United States of America, at the end of 1857. The example was followed by New South Wales in 1864, by Germany in 1868 and by Victoria in 1869. England came only fifth, in 1870. In 1883 there were only 27 countries using stamped wrappers, whereas 224 countries had movable stamps and 65 stamped envelopes. For ten years the number of countries using wrappers has been increasing, it now reaches 51.

As in the case of envelopes, one must examine the stamp and the wrapper which bears it. What I have said of the stamp in relation to the movable stamp, and what

I have said of the stamp in stamped envelopes, is applicable to stamps on wrappers.

The size of the wrappers is varied. The first American ones measured 150 by 250 millemetres—sometimes 255. Those which came after measured 100 by 200 and 125 by 200. In England and in its colonies the measure in general is 125 by 300 millimetres. In France, the wrappers used measure 28 by 5 millimetres.

Wrappers are white, straw, fawn or manilla; the paper is generally plain. Some have a water-mark, the water-mark of the envelopes in the United States, or the letters N. S. W., or the value in letters, or the Kangaroo, in New South Wales.

A certain number of wrappers have a colored border, as in Denmark. As for the values printed on the stamps, they are in general small—1 centime or 2 centimes, half a penny and one penny.

I shall recall that if postal wrappers are of recent origin, revenue wrappers are quite ancient. These have been in use in England for at least two centuries. In America there is a certain number of private stamps which are called proprietary stamps. In France playing cards have been for a long time surrounded with a special gaufered stamp.

CHRONOLOGICAL LIST OF COUNTRIES WHICH HAVE ISSUED STAMPED WRAPPERS.

1, United States of America, end of 1857; 2, New South Wales, April 1, 1864; 3, German Confederation, November 1, 1868, O; 4, Victoria, September 8, 1869; 5, Great Britain, October 1, 1870; 6, Roumania, October 15, 1870; 7, Switzerland, May 18, 1871; 8, German Empire, Dec. 15, 1871; 9, Wurtemberg, January 1, 1872; 10, Denmark, June 1, 1872; 11, Austria, June, 1872; 12, Hungary, Oc-

tober 1, 1872; 13, Bavaria, February 1, 1874; 14, Japan,
April 1, 1875; 15, Guatemala, April, 1875; 16, Canada,
May, 1875; 17, Heligoland. April 1, 1878; 18, **New Zealand**, April 1, 1878; 19, Argentine Republic, November,
1878; 20, Uruguay, January, 1879; 21, Ceylon, end of
1879, 22, Cyprus, April, 1880; 23, Cape of Good Hope,
January, 1881; 24, Republic of San Domingo, September
1, 1881; 25, South Australia, January 11, 1882; 26,
France, October 1, 1882; 27, Barbadoes, October, 1882;
28, English Guiana, February 1, 1884; 29, Trinidad,
August, 1884; 30, Natal, February, 1885; 31, Malta, September, 1885; 32, New Zealand, 1885; 33, Gibraltar, Jan. 1, 1886; 34, Grenada, June 8, 1886; 35, Mexico,
July 1, 1886; 36, Persia, 1886; 37, Bechuanaland, Jan. 1887;
38, Paraguay, March 7, 1887; 39, Santa-Lucia, Dec. 19,
1887; 40, Jamaica, September 1, 1888; 41, Egypt, Jan.
1, 1889; 42, Brazil, January, 1889; 43, French Colonies,
January 1889; 44, Salvador, December 3, 1889; 45, Newfoundland, 1889; 46, Republic of Honduras, Jan. 1, 1890;
47, Nicaragua, Jan. 1, 1890; 48, Russia, January, 1890; 49,
Costa Rica, August, 1890; 50, Finland, May 1, 1891;
51, Leeward Islands, June 1, 1891; 52, Tasmania, 1891;
53, Ecuador, January 1, 1892; 54, Queensland, 1892.

POST CARDS.

If one may judge of the value of an invention by the
rapidity with which its use is extended, it is just to say
that the post card must be placed in the first rank after
movable stamps. According to the journal "L'Amateur" the invention of post cards is due to Dr. Emmanuel
Herrmann who was a professor of National Economy at
the military academy of Wiener-Neustadt.

He published in the "Neue Freie Presse" of July 26,
1869, an article entitled "New Means of Postal Corre-

spondence " in which he developed his ideas on the post card., The general director of the Austrian Post Office, Baron A. Maly, instigated a decree of the Minister of Commerce which created the post card issued October 1, 1869. There were in July, 1883, one hundred and twelve States which had adopted it. It cannot be denied that the post card is the most popular, the most convenient, the most easy and the least costly of all methods of correspondence.

Yet certain countries, like France, seem to have adopted the post card regretfully. The proof of this is the fact that in France the humble card which circulates within the walls of Paris is subjected to the same duty as that which goes to Japan or Australia.

There are two conditions of the post card : First, a single card ; second, a double card with prepaid reply. From the post card is derived the letter sheet.

A—Single Post Cards.

The single post card bears on one side a formula destined for the address and a stamp ; and on the other side a blank for correspondence.

When the first Austrian post card appeared Hungary had no special postal service and its card was distinguished from that of the countries beyond the Leitha only by the Hungarian legend. The first cards measured one hundred and twenty by eigthy-five millemetres. Their use was soon extended into the neighboring countries. All the States of Germany adopted them in 1870 in larger size, one hundred and sixty-four by one hundred and eight. Great Britian and Switzerland followed. In 1871 Belgium, the Netherlands, Denmark, Canada, Chili and Finland adopted the new method of correspondence. Russia, Norway, Ceylon and Sweden accepted it in 1872.

France came only twenty-second, in 1873, after all the great States of Europe, only a few months before the United States, Spain and Italy. The actual size of post cards, fourteen by nine centimetres, is the consequence of the adoption of a uniform type by virtue of Article 15 of the treaty of the Congress of Paris in 1878.

In all cards the recto is reserved for the stamp and address. The stamp, which at first was often lácking, is at the right of the card. The same Article 15 of the treaty of Paris requested that the post card should be stamped.

What I have said of movable stamps and of stamps on envelopes and wrappers is applicable to stamps on post cardᵉ

Several of the first issues of post cards have a frame printed in the same color as the legend. In some countries the coats of arms are printed at the left, as in the Netherlands, or in the middle as in Germany. The title of the post card is in the middle of the card.

This title varies. The first cards of Austria and Germany are inscribed Correspondenz Karte. Those that followed since 1872 are inscribed Post Karte, Carte Postale. It was an article of the treaty of Paris which decided the adoption of the words Post Card instead of Correspondence Card. Cards used for exchange in the Postal Union must bear the title of post card in French, in the language of the country where it is issued and the name of that country.

Under the title are three or four lines for inscription of the address. On the first is printed : An, To, Sr, D., Til, Till, M., A. M., or Czim.

At first the cards bore a notice in several articles in one or two columns of the use to which the card was to be put. Now this notice has been suppressed. A single line tells in the language of each country that the address is to be written on one side of the card and that nothing but the address is to appear there.

The printing of the formula of post cards is made on sheets of various sizes. The result is the simultaneous impression of a certain number. This impression being typographic ordinarily the duplication is made from a single composition. If the impression be lithographic there may be several designs. If there are, one must expect to meet a certan number of varieties in cards resulting from small differences either in titles or in notices.

When post cards are ornamented with frames printed from small blocks one may realize how variety in number of blocks may make differences on cards of various sizes. These differences are varieties that collectors classify.

It is important to note the use of legends in several languages on one card. In Austria, where the official language is German, there were, as early as 1871, a series of post cards for Bohemia and a series for each one of the various provinces. In November, 1869 Hungary cards had a Hungarian legend ; later an Illyrian legend was added. In Turkey cards have a French and a Turkish legend.

The first card of Ceylon has legends in two native languages besides its English legend. Java has a Malay legend in Latin characters, and a Javanese one for cards destined to the interior of the country, besides the Dutch legend, and at Borneo cards have a Chinese and a Malay legend.

The reverse of cards is blank except in certain cards of Ceylon and the Dutch Indies where native legends are inscribed.

The color of post cards has varied. The first cards of

Austria were yellowish. Those of Bavaria are of an
ashy gray color. In England the first post card were
white, and they have become fawn cards. In
France, the first cards had a frame and were at times
white, at times fawn. They bore no stamp, but the place
for a stamp was indicated. They were small, measuring
12 by 8 centimetres. Later they were 14 by 9 centimetres and bore a printed stamp, but no frame and none of
the original notices. The recto was violet, the reverse
was white. In July, 1890, the color was changed to
fawn, and later to pale blue. The fawn color predomin-
ates, but there are green cards in Italy, pink ones in Roumania and in Montenegro. The post cards of the United
States are manilla.

Some post cards have a water-mark. In Bavaria this is
formed of wavy lines as in envelopes and movable
stamps. The water-mark in Hungary forms the letters
M. K. Posta.

B—Double Post Cards.

Double post cards with prepaid reply came after single
cards. The German Empire, in January, 1872, seems to
have been the first to make use of them. The double card
was adopted by the Netherlands in May, 1872; by Belgium and Sweden in January, 1873; by Luxembourg in
February; by Roumania in June; by Servia in July and
by Spain in December; Italy and the Dutch Indies adop-
ed it in 1874, and Switzerland and Finland in 1875.

The formation of the Universal Postal Union caused a
development in the issue of these cards only after several years. The Congress of Berne and that of Paris accepted single cards, but thought the post card with prepaid reply was not useful enough. The congress left to
the several states the faculty to make use of it but did
not admit the obligation to do so. Its use was adopted

several years later by the Congress of Lisbon. Its size has been determined to be that of two single cards.

The card with prepaid reply is formed by the union of two single cards. Only, on one of the cards, is a small notice in the language of the country that the card affixed is for a reply.

The color of the double card is not always identical with that of the single card. In France the color of the double card was blue from its origin in 1879, whereas the single cards of the same epoch were violet lilac on one side and white on the other.

The two leaves which form the card are folded together. In general they are separated by simply tearing them at the fold. To facilitate the division the same processes are used as for stamps, that is, perforation or rouletting.

In double cards it is important to note the situation of the recto in the two leaves with regard to each other. There are double cards in which the reverses face each other. In such cases the cards were printed with one impression. There are other cards wherein the recto of the reply faces the reverse of the original. To print them two processes were required.

Cards, envelopes and wrappers which have been preserved entire are called in France, ''Entiers.'' Thus they are distinguished from collections wherein the stamps only have been preserved. I have always protested against the latter pernicious practice.

CHRONOLOGICAL LIST OF COUNTRIES THAT HAVE ISSUED POST CARDS.

1. SINGLE CARDS.

1, Austria, October 1, 1869; 2, Hungary, Oct. 1, 1869; 3, Alsace-Lorraine, June 25, 1870, O; 4, Bavaria, July 1,

1870; 5, Germany (North Confederation), July 1, 1870,O;
6, Wurtemberg, July 8, 1870; 7, Baden, August, 1870, O;
8, Luxumbourg, September 1, 1870; 9, Switzerland, October 1, 1870; 10, Belgium, January 1, 1871; 11, Netherlands, Jan. 1, 1871; 12, Denmark, August 1, 1871; 13,
Canada, June, 1871; 14, German Empire, July 1, 1871; 15,
Finland, October 1, 1871; 16, Chili, December 23,
1871; 17, Russia, January 1, 1872; 18, Norway, January
1, 1872; 19, Sweden, January 1, 1872; 20, Ceylon, January 1, 1872; 21, Shanghai, January 1, 1873; 22, France,
January 15, 1873; 23, Austrian Levant, January, 1873;
24, Newfoundland, April 1, 1873; 25, United States, May,
12, 1873; 26, Roumania, June 1, 1873; 27, Servia, July 1,
1873; 28, Heligoland, Sept. 1873, O; 29, Spain, December 1, 1873; 30, Japan, December 1, 1873; 31, Italy, January 1, 1874; 32, Dutch Indies, April 1, 1874; 33, Reunion, June, 1874; 34, Great Britain, Oct. 1, 1874; 35, Guatemala, April, 1875; 36, Uruguay, October 10, 1875; 37,
New South Wales, December 1, 1875; 38, Greece, May
20, 1876; 39, Victoria, July 1, 1876; 40, Curacoa, July,
1875; 41, Dutch Guiana, July, 1876; 42, New Zealand, November 1, 1876; 43, South Australia, December, 1876; 44,
Guadeloupe, 1876; 45, French Colonies, 1876; 46, Turkey, January 1, 1877; 47, Jamaica, April 1, 1877; 48,
Danish Indies, September 27, 1877; 49, Cochin-China,
1877: 50, Portugal, Jan. 1, 1878; 51, Azores, Jan. 1, 1878;
52, Maderia, January 1, 1878; 53, Cuba, Jan. 1, 1878; 54,
Cape of Good Hope, January 1, 1878; 55, Porto-Rico,
Jan. 1878; 56, Persia, April, 1878; 57, Nicaragua, July,
1878; 58, Argentine Republic, October, 1878; 59, Egypt,
January 1, 1879; 60, Mauritius, February 15, 1879; 61,
Trinidad, April 1, 1879; 62, Hong-Kong, May, 1879; 63,
Bulgaria, May, 1879; 64, Western Australia, May, 1879;
65, Mexico, June, 1879; 66, English Indies, July 1, 1879;
67, San Domingo, July, 1, 1879; 68, English Guiana, July

3, 1879; 69, Bosnia-Herzegovin a, July, 1879; 70, Phillipine Islands, September, 1879; 71, Saint Christopher, November 18, 1879; 72, Antigua, December 15, 1879; 73, Montserrat, December, 1879; 74, British Honduras, end of 1879; 75, Iceland, end of 1879; 76, Malacca, end of 1879; 77, Nevis, end of 1879; 78, Lagos, end of 1879· 79, Virgin Islands, January, 1880; 80, Gold Coast, Jan. 1880; 81, Eastern Roumelia, Jauuary, 1880; 82, Cyprus, April, 1880; 83, Gambia, July, 1880; 84, Venezuela, August 1880; 85, Bermuda, September 1, , 1880; 86, Brazil, December 2. 1880; 87, Queensland, end of 1880; 88, Hyderabad, end of 1880; 89, Columbia, January 1, 1881; 90, Sierra Leone, January 1, 1881; 91, Republic of San Domingo, January 1, 1881; 92, Tobago, March, 1881; 93, Bahamas, April, 1881; 94, Grenada, April, 1881; 95, Labouan, June, 1881; 96, Santa Lucia, July, 1881; 97, Turk Islands, July, 1881; 98, Hayti, July, 1881; 99, Barbadoes, September 1, 1881; 100, Tasmania, January 1, 1882; 101, Liberia, January 1882; 102, Saint Vincent, January 1882; 103, Paraguay, January, 1882; 104, Republic of Honduras, March, 1882; 105, Hawaii, April, 1882; 106, Martinique, May, 1882; 107, San Marino, July 1, 1882; 108, Portuguese India, December, 1882; 109, Costa Rica, January 1, 1883; 110, Salvador, January, 1883; 111, Siam, July 16, 1883; 112; Jummoo Cashmere, July 1883; 112, Jhind, November, 1883; 114, Peru, end of 1883; 115, Orange, January, 1884; 116, Ecuador, February 9, 1884; 117, Puttiala, October 1, 1884; 118, Senegal, 1884; 119, Angola, Jan. 1, 1885; 120, CapeVerde, Jan. 1, 1885; 121, Portuguese Guinea, Jan. 1, 1885; 122, Malta, January 1, 1885; 123, Mozambique, January 1, 1885; 124, Natal, February, 1885; 125, Gwalior, July 1, 1885; 126, Transvaal, September, 1885; 127, Nabha, July 1, 1885; 128, Bulgaria, September, 1885; 129, Bankok, 1885; 130, Macao Timor, September, 1885; 131, Saint Thomas and Prince, 1885; 132, Gibraltar, Jan-

uary 1, 1886; 133, Congo Free State, January 1, 1886;
134, Montenegro, April 1, 1886; 135, Bechuanaland,
July 1, 1886; 136, Chamba, August, 1886; 137, Faridkot,
January, 1887; 138, Bolivia, May, 1887; 139, Nepal, 1887;
140, Perak, 1887; 141, Montenegro, January 1, 1888; 142,
Tunis, July 1, 1888; 143, Travancore, end of 1888; 144,
North Borneo, June, 1889; 145, German Levant, October
1, 1889; 146, Seychelles, April 5, 1890; 147, Leeward Islands, January 1, 1891; 148, Cook Islands, June 19, 1892;
149, St Pierre and Miquelon, July, 1892; 150, Diego
Suarez, end of 1882; 151, Niger Coast Protectorate, end
of 1892; 152, Erythrea, January 1, 1893; 153, French
Congo, 1893; 154, Ivory Coast, 1893; 155, French
Guinea, 1893; 156, French Guiana, 1893; 157, French Indies, 1893; 158, Indo-China, 1893; 159, Mayotte, January, 1893; 160, New Caledonia, January, 1893; 161, Obock,
January, 1893; 162, Oceanica, January, 1893; 163, Sultanate of Anjouan, January, 1893; 164, Swaziland, January, 1893; 165, Tangier, January, 1893; 166, South Africa, 1893; 167, Zululand, 1893; 168, East Africa, 1893;
169, Benin, 1893.

CARDS WITH RESPONSE.

1, German Empire, January 1, 1872; 2, Bavaria, Janu-
ary 1, 1872; 3, Wurtemberg, February, 1872; 4, Netherlands,
May, 1872; 5, Belgium, January 1, 1873; 6, Sweden,
January 1, 1873; 7, Luxembourg, February 1, 1873; 8,
Roumania, June 1, 1873; 9, Servia, July 1, 1873; 10,
Spain, December 1, 1873; 11, Italy, January 1, 1874; 12,
Dutch Indies, April 1, 1874; 13, Switzerland, June, 1874;
14, Finland, July 10, 1875; 15, Uruguay, October 10,
1875; 16, Heligoland, September 1, 1876, O; 17, Guate-
mala, 1876; 18, Argentine Republic, October, 1878; 19,
Portugal, April, 1879; 20, Azores, April, 1879; 21,
Madeira, April, 1879; 22, Norway, May, 1879; 23,

France, July 1, 1879; 24, Cuba, January 1,1880; 25, Austria, August 1, 1880; 26, Hungary, August 1, 1880; 27, Turkey, December, 1880; 28, Brazil, December 2, 1880; 29, Bosnia-Herzegovina, 1880; 30, Austrian Levant, 1880; 31, Republic of San Domingo, January, 1881; 32, Eastern Roumelia, July, 1881; 33, Paraguay, January, 1882; 34, Honduras (Republic), March, 1882; 35, San Marino, July 1, 1882; 36, Chili, September 9, 1882; 37, Great Britain, October 1, 1882; 38, Liberia, October 18, 1882; 39, Canada, December 20, 1882; 40, Victoria, December, 1882; 41, Curacao, end of 1882; 42 Columbia, end of 1882; 43, New South Wales, January 5, 1883; 44, Salvador, January, 1883; 45, South Australia, March, 1883; 46, Santa Lucia, March 19, 1883; 47, Costa Rica, April, 1883; 48, Jamaica, June 16, 1883; 49, Barbadoes, June, 1883; 50, Greece, July, 1883; 51, Dutch Guiana, July, 1883; 52, Danish West Indies, July, 1883; 53, Sierra Leone, July, 1883; 54, Denmark, July, 1883; 55, Tabago, August 10, 1883; 56, English Guiana, September 1, 1883; 57, Bahamas, September, 1883; 58, Mauritius, October 1, 1883; 59, Iceland, end of 1883; 60, Peru, end of 1883; 61, Trinidad, January, 1884; 62, Hawaii, January, 1884; 63, English Indies, February 1, 1884; 64, Bulgaria, April, 1884; 65, Nicaragau, July, 1884; 66, Montserrat, July, 1884; 67, Gambia, July, 1884; 68, Egypt, November, 1884; 69, Puttiala, 1884; 70, Ecuador, end of 1884; 71, Japan, January, 1885; 72, Malta, January, 1885; 73, French Colonies, April, 1885; 74, Gwalior, July 1, 1885; 75, Jhind, July 1, 1885; 76, Nabha, July 1, 1885; 77, Turk Islands, 1885; 78, Mexico, January, 1886; 79, Malacca, January, 1886; 80, Russia, April 1, 1886; 81, Monaco, April 1, 1886; 82, Grenada, June 8, 1886; 83, Antigoa, 1886; 84, New Zealand, July, 1886; 85; San Domingo, July, 1886; 86, Nevis, 1886; 87, Faridkot, January, 1887; 88, Siam, April 1, 1887; 89, Lagos, July, 1887;

90, Venezuela, July, 1887; 91, Saint Christopher, 1887. 92, Montenegro, January 1, 1888; 93, Tunis, July 1. 1888; 94, Chamba, end of 1888; 95, Congo Free States, March, 1889; 96, Gibralta, March, 1889; 97, Phillipine Islands, July, 1889; 98, German Levant, October 1, 1899; Leeward Islands, January 1. 1891; 100, Bolivia, June, 1891; 101, Bermudas. January, 1892; 102, Ceylon, March, 1892; 103, Hong-Kong, March, 1892; 104, British Honduras, March, 1892; 105, Newfoundland, April 1, 1892; 106, Natal, May 11, 1892; 107, Cape of Good Hope, June, 1892; 108, Travancore, June, 1892; 109, Porto-Rico, July, 1892; 110, prus, July, 1892; 111, Tasmania, July, 1892; 112, United States, October 27, 1892; 113, Bechuanaland, November, 1892; 114, Queensland, end of 1892; 115, Gold Coast, end of 1892; 116 Erythrea, January 1, 1893; 117, Saint Vincent, January, 1893; 118, Macao Timor, January, 1893; 119 Saint Thomas and Prince, January, 1893; 120, Cochin-China. January, 1893; 121, French Congo, January, 1893; 122, Ivory Coast, January, 1893; 123, Guadeloupe, January, 1893; 124, French Guinea, January, 1893; 125, French Guiana, January, 1893; 126, Indo-China, January, 1893; 127, French Indies, January, 1893; 128, Reunion, January, 1893; 129, Martinique, January, 1893; 130, Mayotte, January, 1893; 131, New Caledonia, January, 1893. 132, Obock, January, 1893; 133, Oceanica, January, 1893; 134, Saint Pierre and Miquelon, January, 1893; 135, Senegal, January, 1893; 136, Sultanate of Anjouan, January, 1893; 137, Diego Suarez, January, 1893; 128, Seychelles, March, 1893; 139, Benin, 1893; 140, Zululand, 1893.

LETTER SHEETS.

According to La Libre Parole the letter sheet was invented by a certain Karoly, who complained of the scandalous behavior of the various governments that adopted his invention. His attack will not have a basis, for I remember to have seen at a stationer's in Paris letter sheets like those at present in use long before people talked of letter telegrams, the first issue of which was made in 1879.

The use of the letter sheet came after all methods of applying postage stamps to correspondence. In Belgium, December 15. 1882, appeared the first letter sheet. Uruguay and Brazil followed in 1883, Mexico in 1884, Austria and Hungary in 1886.

The letter sheet measures in France 16 by 13 centimetres. It is folded in two; the side which, after folding, forms the interior is for correspondence ; the exterior has three lines of irregular rouletting at a distance of 9 millemetres from the edge. The stamp is affixed at the right corner. In the middle are inscribed the words Letter Sheet and underneath are four or five lines for the address. At the bottom is a line of notice. The French notice is : To open the letter sheet tear the dotted lines.

The size of the letter sheet varies. It is sometimes 18 by 14 centimetres in size, as in Denmark and in Great Britian and sometimes 19 by 15 as in Victoria.

The folding of the sheet is at the top usually; but in Portugal, in Austria and in certain South American countries the folding is at the bottom.

The rouletted lines are not all at the same distance from the edge. This distance varies from 5 to 9 millemetres Most often the leaves are gummed.

In French post offices one may obtain letter sheets which are not gummed, so that those who buy them may have them copied in their letter books. There is no other method in use to facilitate the opening of the letter sheets than the rouletting.

The intersection of the two rouletted lines, vertical and horizontal causes varieties which certain amateurs collect. The most ancient variety is in two lines that form a cross. This is found in the first letter sheet of Belgium.

In the second variety, one of the lines goes to the edge of the sheet while the other stops at its meeting with the first line.

In the third variety, the two lines stop at their point of intersection and do not reach the edge of the sheet. In a fourth variety, which is found only in the letter sheets of Russia and Finland, the two lines form a convex arc.

The paper of the sheet varies in strength. The color is often uniform on both sides. Ordinarily the exterior is fawn colored, green, gray, azure, pink, pale yellow, while the interior is white or cream or azure. In general, every country adopted an exterior color different for every value; but no rule about this was established by the Postal Union.

Once folded the letter sheet presents a formula composed of a stamp, a legend, several lines for the address and a notice. The stamp has no special characteristics. It is usually placed at the upper right corner. In Portugal and in the Azores it is placed at the left.

The letter sheet of the Austrian post office of Constantinople bears on its stamp the surcharge of the movable stamp of the same value in Turkish money. The letter sheet of the Azores is distinguished by the application of the name Azores as a surcharge on the letter sheet of Portugal.

In some cases, at the left are the coats of arms of the

country, as in Sweden and Denmark, either in black or in the color of the stamp.

All the letter sheets bear the title "Letter Sheet," or its equivalent. As they are single letters the regulations of the Postal Union do not make a double title in French and in local language obligatory. Only the 200 reis of of Brazil, with portrait of Dom Pedro, bears the French title.

Habitually one finds in every country two stamped letter sheets of the two most ordinary postal values. There is a third in Mexico for correspondence between cities where the local postage is different.

The Argentine Republic is the only country which issues a special sheet containing a smaller one for a reply. The latter is united with the first by a metallic thread. The weight of the united sheets is five or six grammes.

In Brazil, the United States and the Netherlands the edge is gummed only at the sides.

CHRONOLOGICAL LIST OF COUNTRIES THAT HAVE ISSUED LETTER SHEETS.

1. SINGLE.

1, Belgium, December 15, 1882; 2, Uruguay, March 1, 1883; 3, Brazil, November 15, 1883; 4, Mexico, November. 1884; 5, Austria, May 1, 1886; 6, Hungary, May 1, 1886; 7, France, June 15, 1886; 8, Bosnia-Herzegovina, July, 1886; 9, United States, August 21, 1886; 10, Austrian Levant, September 15, 1886; 11, Monaco, October 1, 1886; 12, Portugal, April 15, 1887; 13, Azores, April 15, 1887; 14, French Colonies, end of 1887; 15, Argentine Republic, January 24, 1888; 16, Tunis, July 1, 1888; 17, Denmark, October 1, 1888; 18, Netherlands, October 15, 1888; 19, Victoria, January 3, 1889; 20, Italy, August

1, 1889; 21, Sweden, September 15, 1889, 22. Russia, January 13, 1890; 23, San Marino, July 1, 1890; 24, Ecuador, January, 1891; 25, Finland, May, 1891; 26, Roumania, July, 1891; 27, Paraguay, August 15, 1891; 28, Great Britain, February 11, 1892; 29, Liberia, October 15, 1892; 30, Erythrea, January 1, 1893; 31, Cochin China, January, 1893; 32, French Congo, January, 1893; 33, Ivory Coast, January, 1893; 34, Diego-Suarez, January, 1893; 35, Guadeloupe, January, 1893; 36, French Guinea, January, 1893; 37, French Guina, January, 1893; 38, French Indies, January, 1893; 39, Indo China, January, 1893; 40, Reunion, January, 1893; 41, Martinique, Jan. 1893; 42, Mayotte, January, 1893; 43, New Caledonia, January, 1893; 44, Obock, January, 1893; 45, Oceanica, January, 1893; 46, Saint Pierre and Miquelon, January, 1893; 47, Senegal, January, 1893; 48, Sultanate of Anjouan, January, 1893; 49, Benin, January, 1893; 50, Canada, February 21, 1893; 51, Bulgaria, June, 1893; 52, Servia, July, 1893; 53, Spain, 1893.

2. WITH PREPAID RESPONSE.

1, Argentine Republic, May 23, 1888.

Movable stamps, envelopes, wrappers, post cards of various kinds, are not the only means by which postal duties are paid. Postage stamps have been applied on a certain number of formulas which I think useful to make known, at least summarily. But it is well to recall that this work treats only of stamps representing a tax, it does not treat of all that relates to postal service. The absence of a stamp is the characteristic sign of things that do not enter into this study, so I have not considered at all envelopes and cards which are franked.

POSTAL ORDERS.

Two systems have been adopted and used in our time by the various postal administrations that issue money orders.

1. The order is addressed directly by the office that issues it to the office which is to pay it.

2. The order is given to its applicant who sends it himself to the person for whom it is issued, and the office which draws it addresses to the office which is to pay it a notice of its issue, with necessary information for the paying office to verify the identity of the person who presents the order.

Both systems have their defenders. The first is simpler, the second is surer. Both have been admitted by the Universal Postal Union.

The use of money orders is not as old as that of stamps, but it is older than that of post cards. For a long time postal orders were used in Germany only. There formulas were used either on paper or on cards. The formulas on cards had fixed stamps. The custom began in Brunswick and Hanover in 1865 and shortly after collectors began to gather examples of it. I admit that stamped money orders may be collected, but not all the formulas which have been used for money orders.

I shall not enter into a detailed description. I shall say only that the Post Anweisung, which are stamped, bear the stamp of the country and of the epoch at the upper right corner. There are several issues of them. In the middle is the name of the country, then Post Anweisung with the figures of the sum that the order calls for; the name and the residence of the payee and the place where

he lives.   In a column at the left is the word Abchnitt, or
Coupon, or both words, a place for the stamp of the office
which accepts the order, and the name and residence of
the person who sends it.   A double vertical line indicates
the point at which this coupon must be separated.   This
remains with the payee.   On the reverse is the formula
of the receipt to be filled, and the stamp of the distribu-
ting office and other indications interesting only the Post
Office.   These details vary with countries and epochs.

For International orders the proceeding is the same.
At the recto are all the informations relative to the value
of the order, the payee and the issuing office; on the reverse is the receipt.

The colors are varied; pink, fawn, white, cream, green
and gray are the principal ones.

A short notice of the countries which have used orders will give an idea of the interest that there is in them.

Germany, which was the first to issue money orders on
cards, has several kinds of them.

1. Post Anweisung, a money order placed in one office
and payable in another.

2. Post Mandat, and later, Post Auftrag, serving for
the collection by the Post Office of commercial bills.

3. Post Auftrag fur Accept Einholung, a draft for which
the Post Office agrees to obtain the acceptance of the person on whom it is drawn.

4. Vorschuss Post Anweisung, serves for the payment
to its sender of the sum due on a letter or on a package.

Only the Post Anweisung has a stamp; the other three
have none.

In Austria there are:

1. Post Anweisung for remittance of money, with or
without stamp.

2. Post Nachname Karte, similar to the Vorschauss Post Anweisung.

3. Steuer Post Anweisung, the combination of the post card and of the money order. The card bears a 2 kreuzer postage stamp. There are a variety of legends in seven or eight languages, as on the cards and letter sheets.

In Hungary there are:

1. Posta Utalivany, at first in Hungarian and in German, later in Hungarian or Italian, at first without stamp, later with stamp.

2. Posta Utanvetely Jegy, the reimbursing postal card.

3. Steuer Post Anweisung, at first called Adointes, and later Intes.

In Hungary, as in Austria, stamps have been suppessed from orders. These in Bosnia and Herzegovina are simple formulas.

Bavaria and Wurtemberg have adopted stamped orders. In Bavaria, there are four values, the lowest of which has been reserved for soldiers. Wurtemburg has several values also; but here besides the stamped order is the stamped order envelope. The paper is fawn colored.

The Duchy of Brunswick adopted in July, 1865, money orders of a color corresponding to the value of the stamps, issued the same year, stamps of one and two silber groschen printed in black. At the same time the Kingdom of Hanover issued two orders on white cards, with stamps of one and two silvergross, also in black.

In Luxembourg there are a great quantity of simple formulas without stamps for national or foreign correspondence. There is also an envelope of 30 centimes for collection of bills.

This same envelope exists in Switzerland, as well as several stamped orders of various values which are like those of Bavaria and Wurtemberg, proportioned to the value of the sums entrusted to the post office.

In France the postal order without stamp has been adopted for some years for remittances of money to foreign countries.

There is a stamped order of Roumania for 1890. There are white cards without stamps for Denmark; a formula without stamp on yellow paper for Sweden.

There is a variety of new orders called Bons de Poste, on paper in France, on cards in Italy, bearing a fixed stamp, postal and not revenue, serving for National correspondence. They are a variety of bank bills. In France this bill is detached from a stub book. At the upper right corner is a fixed stamp of the value of the order. The name of the payee, which must be inscribed in the middle, and the receipt, complete the similarity of these bills with card orders. They are distinguished from bank bills by the fact that their circulation is limited to three months.

Italy issued in 1890 card orders in nine values, from a fraction of a lire to 20 lires, payable in all offices, and recalling French bills, except by the fact that they are printed on cards instead of paper. Every order has at its right a coupon which the sender keeps; and at the left another coupon sometimes inscribed on its reverse with the address of the payee. In the middle are the title, the arms of Italy and the formula of address. At the top, at the right, is a stamp of 10 centessimi, brownish red, for the first six values, and 15 red, 20 orange and 25 blue for the other values. At the left is the place for the stamp of the sending office. At the reverse is the formula for the receipt. At the place of the address is a background inscribed with the value. The card is varied in color.

The three highest values are on cards, orange, brick, pink, green, pa.e blue, yellow and cream white.

This arrangement seems to have been adopted by a certain number of countries. I learn that such orders are used at Queensland, Victoria and elsewhere. There are few collectors for such orders. A list of the countries that use them follows:

CHRONOLOGIGAL LIST OF COUNTRIES THAT HAVE ISSUED VARIOUS MONEY ORDERS.

I.—MONEY ORDERS NOT STAMPED.

1, Prussia, January 1, 1865, O; 2, Oldenburg, 1865, O; 3, Office Tour and Taxis, January 1, 1866, O; 4, Lubeck, April 1, 1866, O; 5, Luxembourg, July 1, 1866; 6, Bavaria, 1866, O; 7 Hamburg, 1866, O; 8, Bremen, 1866, O; 9, Austria, March 1, 1867; 10, Hungary, March 1, 1867; 11, Germany, (Northern Confederation) January, 1868; 12, Denmark, 1868; 13; Netherlands, November, 1870, 14, Sweden (on paper) November, 1870; 15, German Empire, December 15, 1871; 16, Alsace-Lorraine, 1872, O; 17, Heligoland, 1873, O; 18, Norway, 1877; 19, France, July, 1878; 20, Bosnia-Herzegovina, 1879; 21, Finland, July, 1881.

II.—STAMPED MONEY ORDERS.

1, Brunswick, July, 1865, O; 2, Hanover, August, 1865, O; 3, Hamburg, March 1, 1866, O; 4, Wurtemburg, February, 1867; 5, Switzerland, July 1, 1867; 6, Austria, May 1, 1870; 7, Hungary, February 1, 1871; 8, Bavaria, May, 1874; 9, Luxembourg, October 1, 1877; 10, Montenegro, 1879; 11, German Empire, July 1, 1880; 12,

Roumania, October, 1890; 13, San Marino, August, 1892; 14, Servia, August, 1892.

III.—Stamped Envelopes.

1, Saxony, (not stamped) July 1, 1865, O; 2. Wurtemburg, February, 1867; 3, Bosnia-Herzegovina, 1879.

IV.—Postal Bonds.

1, France; 2, Italy, October 1, 1890.

OTHER STAMPED FORMULAS.

Among stamped postal formulas, I shall note :

1.   Return receipts for Finland, the successive issues of which are stamped with the different postal types that have existed in that country.

2.   The postal savings bank bonds in use in Austria and in Hungary.   They are a species of cards containing 10 or 20 blanks.   One of these is printed with a stamp the value of which is 1 kreuzer.   The postoffice sells the card for that price.   Whenever the owner of the card saves money he invests the sum in postage stamps. When the card is covered the postoffice receives it and registers the amount of the affixed stamps.   They are ordinary postage stamps and differ in this from savings bank stamps which are special stamps in the custody of the postal clerks, and with which they verify the amounts inscribed in the savings bank books.   The savings bank's stamps do not represent a tax nor a duty and should not be collected by amateurs.

3.   Carriage letters have sometimes been postmarked; but the stamp is ordinarily a revenue stamp.

4.   Package cards in use in Italy and in the Republic of San Marino, bear in the first case fixed stamps having the portrait of King Humbert in six different values, three for the interior, three for international correspon-

dence; in the second case stamps with figure of a woman also in six values and types.   The type is the same in each series and placed at the upper right corner.   The rest of the card bears all the necessary information for issue, and formula for the receipt on the reverse.

5.   The postal books of receipts used in Italy, Mexico and Switzerland bear in the first case a movable stamp with portrait of the king on every leaf; in the second case a red stamp of 20 centavos of July, 1886.

I do not consider as postage stamps images which many countries have issued for several years and which have been applied on returned letters.   They are simple seals of gummed paper bearing the name of the country and an explanatory phrase like, "Officially Sealed."   They are not stamps representing a tax.   In the countries where these tickets are not adopted a wax seal is applied.

It is understood that stamps of private postoffices and of railways are the objects of special study.   The stamps of which I have written have been issued by governments and not by societies.

TELEGRAPHIC STAMPS.

Before treating of telegraphic stamps it would be well, perhaps, to understand what telegraph means.   When the Abbe Chappe initiated in France in 1794 the first telegraphic line announcing the capture of Conde the instrument justified its etymology.   It was an instrument for writing from a distance,   For fifty years its use could not be confounded with that of the postoffice.   The telegraph could be used only for despatches of the government because of the slowness in transmission and the cost.   When progress in physical studies demonstrated the great use which could be made of electro-magnetism when Morse invented in the United States in 1844 the first telegraphic line, and Wheatson invented the telegraphic dial, Chappe's invention lost all importance.

I do not intend to retrace here the history of the telegraph. Its nature did not change as its methods were altered. It remained writing from a distance. The despatch card used in France during the siege of Paris was printed on leaves of collodion and carried by pigeons; it was an aerial post or telegraphic line. Since then the pneumatic post whereby the original despatch is transmitted, has been imagined. Paris, London and Berlin use it. The service is directed by the telegraph department.

In later years, in France, the telephone became an adjunct of the postoffice and used special tickets. The analogy was the best reason which could be given for reuniting the two administrations of postoffice and telegraph. This was done in Spain under the name of Comunicaciones.

This leads to a discussion of telegraphic stamps, which, like postage stamps, exist under three principal conditions :

1. Movable stamps, which are affixed to the despatch by the sender at the office.

2. Fixed stamps printed in advance on envelopes, cards, sheets, telegraph notices and receipts.

These two varieties of stamps shall be examined successively through their use in electric telegraph, pneumatic post and telephone. The use of stamps in electric telegraph was begun in 1861. There were two great classes of them, issued by the State or by corporations.

The firsttelegraphic stamps known were made in India. There the stamps measure 60x33 millimetres ; the portrait of the Queen and the face value are represented twice. The stamp is cut in two; the bottom part is affixed to the dispatch, the upper part is affixed on the receipt given to the sender. This is why such stamps are whole only when new, and always cancelled in the upper part. The same usage exists at Ceylon, where the first stamps were those of India, surcharged Ceylon.

The first countries which in Europe made use of mov· able stamps were Prussia, in 1864, and Spain the same year. There the stamps were affixed on the dispatch itself and cancelled by hand. They remained whole; one may find them new ; but one cannot obtain them cancelled.

Forty States have issued telegraphic stamps since 1861, but it must be said that England at first gave the telegraphic service to special corporations, which issued stamps or sheets, and that four nations, the United States, Brazil, Canada and the Republic of San Domingo have retained this method.

Prussia and France have ceased to use telegraphic stamps.

As what I have said of movable postage stamps is applicable to fixed telegraphic stamps, it would be useless to dwell on these. Telegraphic stamps are often only postage stamps surcharged Telegrafos.

Some countries like Russia, Austria, Belgium and Victoria began issuing such stamps as stamped sheets. All did not adopt movable stamps. Some, like Austria, added to them telegraph advices and receipts.

The pneumatic posts made use of stamps only in Vienna, Paris and Berlin ; there sheets, envelopes, single and double cards, letter sheets and return cards are used. The Parisian cards present a plan of Paris, the different tints of which indicate the portions of the city furnished with pneumatic tubes. The cards bear stamps sometimes special and distinct from postage stamps. Yet the first Parisian cards have the legend, "Le Commerce et la Paix," like those of the postoffice.

It seems to me to be an abuse of collecting to classify with telegraphic stamps telephone tickets. These tickets give to subscribers the right to correspond by telephone for a certain time. You give your ticket to a clerk, and no proof remains of your dispatch. The tickets are not movable stamps. They are not cancelled ; they are a seal like the admission ticket which one receives at a play-house office. There is in common between the telegraph and the telephone nothing but transmission from a distance. Telephone tickets are a sort of paper money, not stamps.

CHRONOLOCICAL LIST OF COUNTRIES THAT HAVE ISSUED TELEGRAPHIC STAMPS.

1, English Indies, 1861; 2, Prussia, June 15, 1864, O; 3, Spain, July 1, 1864; 4, Russia, March 4, 1866; 5, Belgium, January 7, 1877; 6, Switzerland, end of 1867, O; 7, France, January 1, 1868, O; 8, Cuba, January 1, 1868; 9, Germany (Northern Confederation) August 1, 1869; 10, Brazil, P. O., September, 1869; 11, Bavaria, January 1, 1870; 12, Porto Rico, January, 1871; 13, Roumania, November 1, 1871; 14, New South Wales, February 1, 1872; 15, Autria, July, 1873; 16, Hungary, August 1, 1873; 17, German Empire, November, 1873; 18, Phillipine Islands, January, 1874; 19, Victoria, January, 1875; 20, Wurtemberg, January 1, 1875; 21, Great Britain, February 1, 1876; 22, Peru, July 1, 1876; 23, Netherland, January 1, 1877; 24, Jamaica, October 20, 1878; 25, Western Australia, 1879; 26, Colombia, January, 1881; 27, United States of America, January, 1881; 28, Ceylon, 1881; 29, Portugal, March, 1882 ; 30, Natal, May 1, 1882 ; 31, Salvador, December 6, 1882; 32, Honduras, January, 1883;

33, Lux mbourg, February 1, 1883; 34, Chili, July 1, 1883; 35, Jummoo Cashmere, January. 1884; 36, Orange, July, 1885; 37, Japan. 1885; 38, Republic of San Domingo, 1886; 39, Argentine Republic, December 8, 1887; 40, Canada, 1887; 41, Cape of Good Hope, 1888; 42, Cordova, 1888; 43, Nicaragua, January 1, 1891; 44, Servia, January, 1891.

REVENUE STAMPS.

Revenue stamps, like postage and telegraphic stamps, come under two conditions : Movable stamps and fixed stamps. The latter class is full of interest. It is the more ancient, and the number of documents which it could show is certainly superior to that of the postage stamps. In France alone the variety of designs in revenue stamps is extraordinary.

The use of movable revenue stamps is much more ancient than that of postage stamps. It would be impossible to tell what country was the first to use them.

There are examples of revenue stamps of Holland in 1579.

In England the Deeds stamps were used in 1694. Fred. George Lundy says in his "History and Chronological Table of the Embossed Deeds Stamps of Great Britain and Ireland" that these stamps were movable, but I do not share his opinion. These stamps were printed one by one on the deeds themselves. The same die served to impress the stamp on paper and on parchment. The stamp was not cancelled because it could not be taken from a document without destroying this.

Medical stamps were probably of the same epoch. The first of them appeared in England in the form of wrappers. They were used to cap bottles. One had to tear them in order to open the bottle.

Until 1850, excepting the gaufered stamps of Holland, the only revenue stamps were fixed or in wrappers.   In 1850, after the postage stamp had become common, the first real movable revenue stamps printed in sheets and in colors, and often rouletted, were issued.   A list which I have made shows that 225 countries issued movable revenue stamps.   This list does not include stamps issued by cities for their special use.

In the first rank figure Austria and Lombardo-Venetia, 1850; Great Britain, 1851 and Spain, 1852.

After what I have written on stamps in general I need not write again of designs, legends, printing, colors and other elements of revenue stamps which are also elements of postage stamps.   I need only refer to the special elements of the former.

The size of the revenue stamp is usually larger than that of the postage stamp.   In Canada the law stamps measure 73x31 millimetres. The life policy stamps in England measure 96x27 millimetres.   Intermediate sizes are common in all countries, but they vary in different epochs in all countries. Thus in France, the first commercial stamps measured 50x25 millimetres; the following ones with the portrait of the emperor measured 45x20 millimetres : the stamps actually in use measure 50x25 millimetres.   The stamps used for posters have varied from 35x5 millimetres to 50x20 millimetres.   Receipt stamps measure 35x19 millimetres.   The first exchange revenue stamps in England measure 58x22 millimetres; now they measure 32x-18.   Several other stamps of England have the same size as those of the postoffice; others are of a much larger size, as for instance the Probate Court matrimonial cause and Chancery Court fee stamps, which measure 30x68 millimetres.

The form is not less variable.   The majority of revenue

stamps are rectangular, but many of them are in the form of triangles, lozenges, ovals and many are irregular.

The designs and legends have portraits, emblems or recall the object of the issue.

It is observed that all the stamps of one issue are of the same color and rarely have two central designs. In France commercial stamps of 1874 have a gray background on which the values are inscribed in blue and in red. The second issue of the empire is slate brown. The value was surcharged in red. In Holland the background was gray, the values to 4.50 florins were inscribed in blue and superior values in red. In the United States the stamps of 1862 had one color for every value; the $200 revenue stamp has a green frame. The center is red. In the series of 1871 the drawing was changed and all the values were printed in blue in a black center. In 1872 the frame of certain values were printed in another color.

In general, revenue stamps are printed by one of the three processes which I have described, but a certain number of them are gaufered on white paper. Such were the stamps of Holland issued after 1579. The paper is usually white, but there are colored examples of gaufered paper. In the United States some series of revenue stamps are on tinted paper.

The design of many postage stamps is admired, but the revenue stamps of Austria are much more remarkable than any for their art of composition, the fineness of the work and its variety. Revenue stamps are usually printed on paper, but some in England are printed on parchment. The operation is difficult and necessitates the use of a zinc leaf submitted to a strong pressure which it communicates to the parchment through a stamp on blue paper.

In the United States there is another class of revenue

stamp formed of zinc leaves covered by a gilt impression, representing a stamp, and used as tobacco wrappers.   It is also for tobacco that interesting specimens of wrappers are issued in the United States.

As regards value revenue stamps present the highest denominations.   In America, in 1862 and 1871, were issued $200 stamps.   I have in my collection the photograph of a $500 American stamp.   The central part is red, the frame is blue.   There is a $5,000 stamp, orange, green and black, the use of which was of course very limited.   In India the highest value of Court Fee stamps is 1000 rupees or $500.   Costa Rica has a stamp of 100 pesos; Mexico a stamp of 1000 pesos.   England must have the palm for revenue stamps of high value.   Deeds stamps of hundreds of pounds sterling, used on wills, are very frequent.

Movable revenue stamps are used for a great variety of objects.   It must be noted that in most important and ancient countries fixed stamps are used ; but other countries, like France, use movable stamps for documents of foreign countries.   The movable stamp replaces advantageously, for instance, the consular visa.

The commercial stamps of Belgium present two series of duties, according to origin and destination and Switzerland has visa stamps.   Stamps for receipts, railways, etc., inspired the idea of creating revenue stamps.   The existence of series of fixed stamps makes the use of movable stamps unnecessary and is a better guarantee against fraud.

In certain countries a single series of stamps is used for the greatest number of duties under names which designate at times the stamp in general—Imposto do Sello, Stempel marke, Timbre nacional—at times the reason for the stamp—Stamp Duty, Revenue Duty, Revenue Stamp; State Revenue, Contribucion, Renta provin-

cial, Impuesto—at times the lawful issue of the stamp—
Stamp Statute—at other times the origin of the stamp—
Internal Revenue, Inland Revenue, Impuesto directo.
In most countries, however, stamps are used only fo
determined objects. Witness for example England where
are found stamps of:

Admiralty Court, Bankruptcy, Board of Agriculture,
Chancery Court, Chancery Fee Fund, Civil Service, Con-
non Law Court, Companies Registration, Consular Service, Contract Note, Copyhold and Commission, Cus-
toms, District Audit, Draft, Foreign Bill, Inland Revenue,
Judicature Fees, Land Commission, Land Registry, Life
Policy, Matrimonial Cause Fee, Naturalization, Patent,
Paymaster General Service, Perfumery Duty, Police Court,
Marine Policy Insurance, Probate Court, Public Records,
Receipt, Transfer Duty, Winding-up Companies. There
are also wrappers for tobacco, coffee and medicine;
there are special stamps for Ireland, Scotland and the Isle
of Man.

Among revenue stamps those used for tobacco, liquors,
beer and many specialties are for the most part in the
state of wrappers. The United States present numerous
series of tobacco stamps interesting by variety in designs
and portraits. Japan's tobacco wrappers are dazzling in
color. Russia's tobacco wrappers are ancient but not
remarkable. The use of movable stamps for revenue
taxes is increasing day by day.

CHRONOLOGICAL LIST OF COUNTRIES THAT HAVE ISSUED REVENUE STAMPS.

By reason of the quantity of revenue stamps used for
many revenue duties, I have indicated only the date of
issue of the first variety created.

1, Austria, September 15, 1850; 2, Lombardo-Venetia,

September 15, 1850; 3, Great Britain, January, 1851; 4, Spain, January 1. 1852; 5, Modena, February 1, 1853, O; 6, Parma, Fabruary 1, 1853, O; 7, Hesse-Cassel, July 24, 1853; 8, Ireland, 1853; 9, Cape of Good Hope, 1854; 10, Natal, 1854; 11, Tessin (Canton), June 8, 1855; 12, Jamaica, November 28, 1855: 13, Spanish Colonies, January 12, 1856; 14, Ceylon; March, 1856: 15, Belgium, September 1, 1857; 16, Zurich (Canton), December 17, 1857; 17, California, December, 1857; 18, Colombia, September 1, 1858: 19, Cundinamarca, 1859; 20, Basle (Canton), January, 1860; 21, Geneva (Canton), January 1, 1860, O; 22, Tuscany, January 1, 1860; 23, France, January 18, 1860; 24, English Indies, November 25, 1860; 25, Magdalena, 1860; 26, Tolima, 1860; 27, Bolivar, January 1, 1861; 28, New Zealand, January, 1861; 29, Sardinia, April 1, 1861; 30, Portugal, December 10, 1861; 31, Azores, December 10, 1861; 32, Madeira, December 10, 1861; 33, Denmark, April 1, 1862; 34, Freiburg (Canton), July 25, 1862; 35, Prussia, September 2, 1862; 36, United States, October 1, 1862, 37; Valais (Canton), November 25, 1862; 38, Senegal, 1862; 39, New Caledonia, 1862; 40, Bremen, January 1, 1863; 41, Italy, January, 1863; 42, Tasmania, November 1, 1863; 43, Mexico, 1863; 44, Portuguese Colonies in Africa, January, 1864; 45, Vaud (Canton), May 1. 1864; 46, Sweden, July 1, 1864; 47, Canada, October 1, 1864; 48, Phillipine Islands, 1864; 49, Porto Rico, January, 1865; 50, Nevada, May, 1865; 51, Berne, June 16, 1865, O; 52, New South Wales, July 1, 1865; 53, Cauca, 1865; 54, Finland, 1865; 55, Corea, 1865; 56, Gaudeloupe, 1865; 57, Martinique, 1865; 58, Cuba, January 6, 1866; 59, English Guiana, March 5, 1866; 60, Louisiana, March 22, 1866; 61, Queensland, 1866; 62, Alabama, February 9, 1867; 63, Puebla, July, 1867; 64, Luxembourg, December 15, 1867; 65, Bolivia, 1867; 66, Hong-Kong, 1867; 67, Malacca, 1867; 68, Orange, 1867; 69, Gautemala, January 1868; 70,

Reunion, April 1, 1868; 71, Saxony, July 15, 1868; 72, Hungary, Aug. 1, 1868; 73, Hesse-Darmstadt, Oct. 1, 1868; 74, Oldenburg, October 12, 1868; 75, Birkenfeld, 1868 ; 76, Nova Scotia, 1868; 77, Spanish West Indies, Jan'y., 1869; 78, Mauritius, March 28, 1869; 79, Buenos Ayres, April, 12, 1869; 80, Brazil, May 15, 1869; 81, Quebec, Sept., 1869; 82, Germany (Northern Confederation), December 30, 1869, O; 83, Victoria, 1869; 84, Caracas, April 19, 1870; 85, Schumberg-Lippe, June 1, 1870; 86, Monserrat, June 16, 1870; 87, Rhepal, 1870; 88, Costa Rica, 1870; 89, Oregon, January 1, 1871; 90, Venezuela, January 1, 1871; 91, Uruguay, February 8, 1871; 92, German Empire, June 8, 1871; 93, Brunswick, July 1, 1871; 94, Ontario, August 1, 1871! 95, Scotland, 1871; 96, Schwartzburg-Sondershausen, June 20, 1872; 97, French Guiana, August 16, 1872; 98, Roumania, September 15, 1872; 99; Norway, November 30, 1872; 100, Afghanistan, 1872; 101, Dutch Guiana, 1872; 102, Japan, 1872; 103, Greece, September 15, 1873; 104, Mecklemburg-Schwerin, January 1, 1874; 105; Mysore, February 21, 1874; 106, Antigua, 1874; 107, Morelos, 1874; 108, Turkey, 1874; 109, Russia, July 1, 1875; 110, Baden, October 1, 1875; 111, Berars, 1875; 112, Manitoba, 1875; 113, Bavaria, Jan. 1, 1876; 114, Grenada, Jan. 1, 1876; 115, Sarawak, 1876; 116, Transvaal, 1876; 117, Entrerios, January 1, 1877; 118, Griqualand, January, 1877; 119, Hawaii, January, 1877; 120, Kappurtala, 1877; 121, Wurtemburg, 1877; 122, Saint Gall, January 1, 1878; 123, Chili, January 10, 1878; 124, Argentine Republic, January 1, 1878; 125, Neufchatel, March 1, 1878; 126, Nevis, end of 1878; 127, Cyprus, end of 1878; 128, San Domingo, end of 1878; 129, Coahuila, end of 1878; 130, Mozambique, end of 1878; 131, Santander, end of 1878; 132, Lichtenstein, January 1, 1879; 133, Santa Fe, January 1, 1879; 134, Angola, January, 1879; 135, Cape Verde, January, 1879;

136, Corientes, January, 1879; 137, Lucerne, January, 1879; 138, Bulgaria, May, 1879; 139, Bosnia-Herzegovina, July 1, 1879; 140, Portuguese Indies, 1879; 141, Macao, 1879; 142, Saint Thomas and Prince, 1879; 143 San Luis, end of 1879; 144, Sirmoor, end of 1879; 145, Tobago, July 1, 1880; 146, East Roumelia, July 15, 1880; 147, Bahawulpoor, 1880; 148, Bikanir, 1880; 149, Limree, 1880; 150, Servia, April 13, 1881; 151, Montenegro, July 1, 1881; 152, Santa Lucia, November 15, 1881; 153, Republic of San Domingo, end of 1881; 154, Cordova, January 1, 1882; 155, Santiago del Estero, January 1, 1882; 156, West Australia, January, 1882; 157, Hayti, January, 1882; 158, Leeward Islands, June, 1882; 159, French Indies, July, 1882; 160, Saint Vincent. September 15, 1882; 161, Portuguese Guinea, 1882; 162, Paraguay, January, 1883; 163, Faridkot, 1883; 164, Michoacan-de-Ocampo,, 1883; 165, Saint Christopher Nevis, 1883; 166, Salvador, 1883; 167, Siam, 1883; 168, Stellaland, January, 1884; 169, New Brunswick, April, 1884; 179, Ecuador, September 1, 1884; 171, Antioquia, 1884; 172, Mendoza, January 1, 1885; 173, Anhalt, January, 1885; 174, Guerrero, July 1, 1885; 175, Guanacaste, November, 1885; 176, Fiji, 1885; 177, Dutch Indies, January 1, 1886; 178, Persia, March, 1886; 179, Argovia (Canton), 1886; 180, Cochin-China, 1886; 181, Holkar, 1886; 182, North Borneo, 1886; 183, Nowanuggur, 1886; 184, San Juan, 1886; 185, Trinidad, January, 1887; 186, Bhanagar Burbar, 1887; 187, Boyaca, 1887; 188, Sierra Leone, 1887; 189, Travancore, 1887; 190, Tucuman, 1887; 191, Monaco, January 1, 1888; 192, Zug (Canton), January 1, 1888; 193, Jalisco, January, 1888; 194, Schwitz, July 1, 1888; 195, Panama, 1888; 196, Rajpeepla, 1888; 197, Selangor, 1888; 198, Jujuy, 1889; 199, La Rioja, 1889; 200, Morvee, 1889; 201, Nicaragua, 1889; 202, Annam, January, 1890; 203, Diego Suarez, August 1, 1890; 204, Eastern Africa,

end of 1890; 205, Catamarca, end of 1890; 206, H yder-
abad, end of 1890; 207, Perak, end of 1890; 208, Zulu
land, end of 1890; 209, Isle of Man, January, 1891; 210,
French Congo, March 1891; 211, Para, July, 1891; 212,
Gibraltar, 1891; 213, Salta, 1891; 214, Egypt, January 1,
1892; 215, Bahia, 1892; 216, San Paulo, 1892; 217, Rio
de Janeiro, 1892; 218, Sabant Vadi, 1892; 219, Central
Africa, 1892; 220, Rio Grande del Sul, April, 1893; 221,
Zanzibar, 1893; 222, Ceara, 1893; 223, Alagoa, 1893; 224
British Columbia, 1893; 225, Parana, 1893.

MUNICIPAL AND PRIVATE STAMPS.

I have considered until now only stamps issued by
governments. I shall undertake to treat of municipal
and private stamps which serve for postage, telegraphic
or revenue duties. There are doubts about the authenticity of many of them, but they are interesting and the
real among them shall be distinguished from the counterfeit.

Among postage stamps one should note in the first
place those of offices of Hamburg. One must admit the
existence of the stamps of C. Hamer & Co., movable
stamps and envelopes; but reject the stamps of H.
Scheerenkeck, W. Krantz, Hamonia & W. Lafranz, which
are fanciful. The issue made by Vandiemen has a business air, but the others were special delivery rather than
post office stamps.

Norway and Denmark have special city stamps, but all
of them were not authentic. The majority of stamps of
the local post offices of Russia are real; but some have
been manufactured expressly for collectors, and they
should not be collected. There are many stamps of
newspaper carriers in England.

In France only the stamps of one society, "Transports
Parisiens" may be found.

The United States contain more private stamps of postage than any other country.   Before the first issue by the government several corporations had been formed for the express purpose of carrying letters to the principal cities.   Adams & Co., Blood & Co., Hale & Co., Hussey & Co. and many others issued special stamps, which disappeared as soon as the first official issue was made.

During the war of secession a certain number of local post offices were established in the Confederate States to take the place of the government service.   But of these two varieties of local post offices a great number of stamps have no more value than the stamps of the offices of Hamburg or of Norway.

In the thirty latest years were circulated in the territories of the United States a great number of stamped envelopes bearing, beside the stamp of the United States or of Mexico, the stamp of a private office which carried letters of miners to regions unprovided with post offices. The best known of these stamps are Wells, Fargo & Co's.

In countries where private corporations took charge of telegraphic lines at the beginning there are corporation stamps.   Thus in England, until 1876, when the government took charge of the telegraphic service.

There are revenue stamps issued by municipalities for the duties which they are authorized by law to charge, as Etat-Civil, Secretariat, Controle, Conciliation, etc.   There are quantities of such stamps in Italy.

Spain and Madrid have an almost annual series of municipal stamps for posters and other duties.   In France there are municipal stamps of Cannes, Epinal, Mans. In England there are municipal stamps of London, Gloucester, Northampton, Southampton, etc.

Private corporations which have issued stamps for duties that belong to them by law are not extant in many countries.   In Spain there are Chambers of Notaries and Lawyers which collect such duties.

The United States issue a series of stamps manufactured by the government for the account of private persons. These are private stamps.   When the war of secession occured in 1861, the necessity of creating revenue led Congress to establish the revenue stamps of 1862. Among them the Playing Card and Proprietary stamps must be noted.   The government issued series of stamps bearing these titles.   They were applied to playing cards, medicine, matches, and served to pay the duties on them. The government permitted also the use of special stamps that none other than their proprietors could have.   Business firms paid for the engraving of a plate bearing a special legend.

All packages, boxes or bottles containing either matches, medicine, perfumery or playing cards, bore a stamp cancelled either by the proprietor's signature or by the fact that the package could not be opened without tearing the stamp.   There are hundreds of such stamps on four kinds of paper : 1, thin paper; 2, paper studded with small threads; 3, pink paper; 4, paper with a water mark U. S. I. R.   As the design was left to the fantasy of the owner and the engraving was entrusted to the American Bank Note and other companies, such stamps have in great variety portraits, legends, eagles of all forms and subjects of all kinds, graceful and delicate, which deserve a collector's best attention.   These stamps have been suppressed the tax having been abolished; but there are none like them anywhere else.   All are inscribed with the amount of their value, the name of the proprietor and the words, "U. S. Internal Revenue." One should not confound them with simple factory marks, which have not the same finish in design nor any indication of value.

All the stamps that I have enumerated are manufactured by the same processes as the national stamps. However, lithography is the process most generally used. It is the most economical.

Usually the design of these stamps is coarse; often different colors of paper distinguish different values. The rouletting is not always well done. There is one signal exception to this generalization; the private stamps of the United States may be known at a glance by the excellence of their manufacture. I will add that they appear in the form of movable stamps, ordinarily, and also in the form of envelopes like those of Wells, Fargo & Co., in wrappers and in cards.

THIRD PART.

GENERALTIES ABOUT STAMPS.

Cancellation of Stamps.

The stamp, whatever may be its object, postal, telegraphic or revenue, is finished and ready for service. The public has bought it; you have affixed the movable postage stamp on the envelope of your letter, or used the stamped envelopes, the wrappers or the cards issued by the government. The business man, the lawyer or the agent of the government has used on his documents the stamps which were printed for them. How is the government to prevent their being used a second time? This question deserves a short study.

At first, when stamps were fixed on stamped paper, the mere fact of writing on the sheet cancelled the stamp. One could not cut off the stamp of one sheet in order to use it on another sheet. This is the rule for envelopes, wrappers and cards. To prevent fraud governments exchange the sheets which are spoiled for movable stamps. So the stamp was cancelled formerly by a mark of the

pen on the value.   Respect prevented the marking of the
portrait. Prussia carried this respect to excess, but other
countries cancelled fixed in the same manner as movable
stamps.

How are stamps cancelled?   In general they are cancelled by means of a hand stamp.   The forms of it are
varied.   The most ordinary, known as a dating stamp, is
formed of two concentric circles between which is in
scribed the name of the city where the letter was posted
and the post office number.   In the middle, in several
lines are the date, the day, the month, the year and often
the hour at which the letter was mailed.   This cancellation appears in innumerable varieties, since it occurs in all
countries, and every post office has its own style of cancellation.

Often the lower circle is lacking ; the dating stamp is
often replaced by a circle or by a series of concentric circles forming a sort of target, the bull's eye of which is
the number of the post office.   At times the outer circle
is indented.   At times the cancellation stamp instead of
being circular is oval; at times it is a horizontal bar.
It may be square, rectangular or polygonal.   It
may be composed of simple inscriptions on two or
three straight or curved lines, or of bars variously arranged with big office numbers in the form of an oval or
of a lozenge.   There are cancellations formed of lines,
straight, wavy, but parallel; of lines forming squares and
lozenges. The Bavarian cancellations have a special form;
two concentric circles united by lines perpendicular to the
circles.

Those whom these various forms interest may consult
with profit the work of M. A. Reinheimer, entitled "Catalogues of German Cancellations from 1849 to 1875 with
1300 illusrations."

The cancellations recorded in this work are not the

only ones that one may find. I do not intend to describe them all. I must mention, however, those which are found on the stamps ef Sicily. They are arabesques on three sides forming a sort of frame. The cancellation is on the frame of the stamp. It leaves intact the central part containing the King's portrait.

A more important question is relative to the ink used for cancellation. Most ordinary inks may be erased by chemical processes. It is therefore necessary to use one which will resist washing. This question has seriously preoccupied all postal administrations since the first stamp was issued.

In France, by the terms of a circular dated December 10, 1848, the cancellation of postage stamps was effected by means of a dated stamp smeared with ink. This ink was probably easily removed. Several chemists called the attention of the administration to this fact. In January, 1849, it was noted that dates were inadequately marked and postal agents were instructed to use printing ink. Where this ink was not easily obtained the clerks were instructed to cancel stamps by means of a large cross " through the blank space in the small figure of the Republic."

The Post Office instructions said, among other things, " In presence of numerous omissions of cancellations it has been decided that every failure of clerks to cancel stamps shall entail a fine of five francs."

This fine was abolished by Cocheris, January 15, 1878. The Post Office instructions above quoted said:

" The cancelling stamp announced in this circular shall be received by the agents this month. It represents a grilled lozenge. Agents must not employ another ink than that which is furnished by the administration and they must not modify it by addition of oil, the chemical composition of this ink being the same as that of the ink used for the printing of the figures, so that any attempt to wash out the ink would result in washing out the vignette at the same time."

A circular dated January, 1, 1852, substituted for the lozenge stamp a cancelling stamp of a new model, the surface of which was armed with conic points that penetrated into the paper. This stamp bore at its centre a conventional number corresponding to the alphabetical classification of the office, so that one could recognize by the stamp the origin of the letter. For Paris the numbers were replaced by initials. The sizes of the central number varied in different years so that it is possible to determine by the size of the central figure whether a stamp was issued before 1852 when the figures were small, or since 1852 when the figures were enlarged. The presence of the grilled lozenge on a stamp is an evidence that it was used from 1849 to 1852. Stamps cancelled with an anchor instead of a number were used on letters coming from across the ocean in packet boats. The circular announcing them is dated June 1, 1857.

October 5, 1860, the Director-General of the French Post Offices decided that the cancellation of figures on stamps "shall be made by means of the dating stamp of the sending office. Postal card stamps must be annulled by means of a cancelling stamp."

Since March, 1876, all French postage stamps, without distinction, have been annulled by means of the dating stamp, a machine invented by Daguin, which makes a double imprint, on the stamp and on the superscription.

The washing out of cancellations has been effected by means of alcohol, ether, benzine, and even sulphate of carbon. The latter chemical takes off the color of the stamp as well as the black of the cancellation. Post office administrations have tried to prevent the fraud by means of :

1. Printing ink.

2. An ink similar to that which was used on the stamps, so that the washing out of a cancellation inevitably entailed that of the design.

3. A stamp studded with conic points which pierce the paper. This method has given the best results. It is almost impossible to clean French, English and Belgian stamps. Yet there are instances where it was done. A certain Jobart, of Brussels, used the same stamp twenty times.

Inks of various colors, blue, red, violet and black, are used. Many are easily effaced, but black printing ink is the most tenacious. The special ink employed by the French administration was invented by the celebrated chemist Dumas.

The work published by Philbrick & Westoby, "The Postage and Telegraphic Stamps of Great Britain," calls attention to an interesting fact on the cancellation of the first English stamps. By a circular of April 25, 1840, signed by the secretary of the general post office, all directors and sub-directors were expressly ordered to cancel stamps with a seal having the form of a sort of cross and to use a special ink, the formula of which was given as follows :

1 pound of red printing ink.

1 pint of linseed oil.

½ pint of sweet oil.

The English post office, like that of other countries, preferred printing ink. The choice of red color doubtless resulted from the fact that the one penny black and the Mulready covers and envelopes were printed with black ink.

The Russian post office used a process which made the

erasing of cancellations impossible. The sheet on
which the stamps were to be printed was covered
with a thin coating of zinc diluted in water. When the
stamp is put in water the dilution of the background en-
tails that of the color. This fact was formerly explained
by the use of aniline colors soluble in water, but Maury
gave the real explanation in an essay full of interesting
information on the first envelopes and stamps of Russia.

Besides cancellation with a seal covered with ink, several processes have been proposed, all of which have for
their object the destruction, or at least alteration, of
stamps. A list of the propositions made to the French
post office, and rejected, is interesting.

Charrier proposed in 1850 a process consisting of printing stamps on seals. There are specimens of the blue
20 centimes with portrait of the Republic printed in this
form. The fragility of seals and their easy alteration by
heat, dryness and dampness has caused this proposition
to be rejected.

The following year the same inventor proposed the application on the back of stamps of a colored silk thread,
the drawing of which would entail the tearing of the
stamp. There are stamps of 20 centimes with portrait of
the Republic and of 5 centimes with portrait of the Emperor, bearing such silk threads in various colors.

Meilhet and Pichot proposed in 1850 the use of a water-
mark manufactured by them. The stamps were to be
printed with two different inks. The application of a
brush dipped in a solution composed of nitric acid and
water caused decomposition of the color. There are
numerous specimens of stamps with portrait of the Republic and that of the President, before cancellation and
showing the results of the use of the brush.

In 1857 Morel proposed a stamp formed of two parts
separated by a straight line rouletted. The upper part

was affixed to the letter, the lower part was separated at the line traced by the roulette.

Lanet de Limancy proposed in 1852 a thin paper for a white background stamp, the cancellation of which radiated from the center.   But the paper was too thin for typographic impression.

In 1855 Muller proposed printing with thin ink soluble in water.

In 1851 Fiche proposed a cancelling stamp which incised postage stamps with stars and circles.

In 1855 Spiers offered a cancelling stamp which cut postage stamps in straight lines.

It is needless to say that all these processes were inadequate.

One of the latest projects consisted in the application on the reverse of stamps of a wafer of fulminate which when struck would destroy the stamp; but the wafer also destroyed the letter.

In 1866 France proposed stamps printed on a very fine substance.   The gum was applied on the printed side. When one removed the stamp from the letter one destroyed it.   The color was fixed to the gum.

The first tax stamps of Prussia and French proofs bearing the portrait of Napoleon III. were made by this decalcomanic process.

Cancellation of stamps is generally effected with a hand stamp.   But when a considerable number of letters are to be cancelled in a short time the utility of machinery is obvious.   The central office in New York uses a machine which strikes at the same time a dated stamp and a cancellation formed of seven straight parallel lines.

I have written on the choice to be made between new and cancelled stamps in collections.   I have shown that cancellation is not a guarantee of authenticity.   All counterfeit stamps are cancelled. I shall return to this question when writing of counterfeit stamps.

It would be useful to demonstrate the authenticity of cancellations. Reinheimer has tried it. His works are useful, but the illustrations which they contain are themselves only imitations to be accepted under reserve. I do not wish to discourage amateurs who study these dry subjects; I acknowledge that they may render great services. If other information be lacking the cancellation stamp may indicate the date of issue, but this not at all sure.

SURCHARGES.

The use of surcharges on stamps has been multiplied in recent years, so much so that collectors have protested against the abuse of them. The Vicomte de Mere wrote : "We have witnessed impassively the successive unloading of cargoes of surcharges, coarser and coarser, of incredible vignettes, and of an assortment of stamps with absolutely unknown silhouettes."

Criticizing an ordinance of the administrators at Nossi-Be, the Timbre-Poste says : "This ordinance lacks seriousness. Like others it exists only to facilitate the sale of stamps sent almost exclusively to Paris to be sold for the benefit of those who print them."

It is almost impossible to obtain stamps of Madagascar and of Diego Suarez. The reason is that the relative of a stamp dealer of Paris has influence with the official authorities in Madagascar and causes all the surcharges to be made for his benefit. Some have gone through the post office, but most of them have not.

There are various classes of surcharges : I shall set aside those which are in a manner complementary to the stamp. Thus Marco del Ponta has shown that in Mexico until 1884 all stamps bear one of two surcharges, name of city, or figures of date. In Mexico, until 1884, it was only through error that stamps were not surcharged.

Similar are the surcharges applied on stamps of French colonies, indicating the place where a stamp was sold and preventing its being sent to another colony where the rate of exchange made the value higher. Nothing can be more legitimate, but the application of surcharges different in size or form of letters is often done in colonies of small population for no other reason than to exploit collectors. Such are the surcharges of Obock, straight and curved, on forty stamp values. Nothing justifies them. At certain epochs in the United States and Peru a gaufered grill was used as a surcharge; at Salvador a "Contra cello" stamp was used; at Porto Rico a flourish, in Servia a monogram. Such surcharges affect neither the value nor the use of stamps. The only evil is that an abuse is made of them. Only the surcharges which modify one of the elements discussed in this work are to be noted ; the principal ones are as follows :

First category.—The surcharge has for its object to create a new value by reason of a change in the postal tariff. For instance, in Italy, in 1865, the 15 centesimi was transformed into a 20 centesimi. To this category belongs the 20 centime blue stamp surcharged 25 in red, prepared in France in 1849 and never put into service. It is probably one of the first stamps with surcharge, but it interests only amateurs of proofs.

Second category.—The existence of a single plate in a country has served as an excuse to print stamps in as many colors as values. The primitive value is scratched and the new value is added as a surcharge. Thus are stamps of Saint Helena.

Third category.—A change in the currency has com-
pelled the administration, while waiting for new stamps,
to apply surcharges on old stamps.   This happened in
Mauritius in 1878.   As all the stamps of one series are
not equally circulated, it is easy to understand that those,
the stock of which was larger, have given rise to surcharges in several values.   In the same category are
surcharges applied for economy's sake on cards, as in
Italy.

Fourth category.—Negligence of administrations, acci-
dents at sea, or other causes resulting in the absence
of certain values, have made necessary the use of surcharges.   The Phillipine Islands and several French colonies have been thus affected.

At all events surcharges on values may have serious
reasons for their existence and to protest against them is
like fighting windmills.   It is noticeable that in most cases
the new value is lower than the original one and that if
there be a loss it falls upon the administration which
gives stamps of 25 centimes, for example, surcharged on
stamps of 1 franc, and stamps of 5 centimes surcharged
on stamps of 40 centimes.

Fifth category.—There are surcharges not on the value
but on the name of the country.   Certain countries lacking stamps have borrowed series of them from neighboring countries.   They have appropriated them through
the application of a name and a special sign.   Such are
the first stamps of Monserrat, 1 and 6 pence, the name of
which is applied as a surcharge on stamps of Antigoa
having the same value, and such are the first stamps of
the Straits Settlement formed by the application of the
royal crown and of the value on stamps of India.   Often
the printing of the name serves only to prevent the use of
the stamp in a country which uses the same stamp before
surcharged.   Such are the stamps of Mysore, Johore, etc.

At Madeira and the Azores the reason of the surcharge is to prevent the loss to the treasury by difference in exchange.

Sixth category.—Spain has printed Habilitado por la Nacion on stamps of Isabella in 1868 and 1869, as a surcharge, in the interval preceding the manufacture of new stamps.

Seventh category.—Surcharges may transform the use of stamps. The application of the word revenue indicates the transformation of postage stamps into revenue stamps. The word Habilitado para Correos in use in the Phillipine Islands has permitted the use for postage of stamps originally printed for another use.

Such are the principal categories into which all surcharges may be divided. In the considerable number of surcharges known are many which are false. But all those which I have enumerated have been used by governments. A collector must therefore obtain them. The collector exacts only that his stsmps should be authentic. He should be able to distinguish false from real surcharges.

1. Every surcharge modifying the value, the name of the country or the use of the stamps must have been preceded by a decree or by an ordinance prescribing it. It may be said that to-day there is not one country using postage stamps and not having one or several collectors. It is the duty of these to transmit to stamp journals copies of decrees or of ordinances. They should do more. They should send the number, the date and all other details of the decree or ordinance.

2. When these details are lacking presumptive evidence may be given. The surcharges made for English colonies are often in Egyptian characters and made methodically. These are easy to recognize; but all stamps surcharged in English colonies are not in that

state. One has only to compare the surcharges on
stamps of Ceylon of 1880 with those of 1884 to realize that
the first ones are not in Egyptian characters. They are
a product of the native industry, and yet their existence
is not contested.

It must be noted also that in several colonies surcharges are made with deficient characters. The only
way for an amateur to recognize a real surcharge from a
false one is to refer to the identical reproductions which
are given in serious catalogues like the seventh edition of
Moen's and Scott's standard Catalogues. In these the
reproductions obtained by photogravure are absolutely
identical. Any description of types taken from a catalogue of fonts is useless. Names vary with countries
and with factories of one country. All measurement is
useless. There is nothing to do but to compare.

3. No decree may have been issued and yet the surcharge may be authentic. When a change in the postal
tariff compels the creation of a new value, a temporary
surcharge is inevitable. It is enough to prove its authenticity that it is soon followed by a new stamp, without
surcharge, of the new value. Witness the Cape 3 pence.
Is not this an indirect proof of authenticity of the stamp
without surcharge? When a new series appears which
contains no value corresponding to that with surcharge
previously offered, one may affirm that the surcharge is a
counterfeit. This is why I have doubted the surcharge
of Cuarto of Colombia.

4. This leads me to note another reason for doubting
surcharges. When a fault is constant, it cannot be explained except by a counterfeiter's ignorance. The Co-
lombian stamps of 4 centavos, 1883, bear the word Cuarto
instead of Cuatro. No decree has been quoted establish-
ing the surcharge; the series of 1883, issued a few months
after, does not contain a 4 centavos stamp; moreover,

there is a fault. Cuarto centavos might mean a quarter of a centavo, if there were no s, but would not mean 4 centavos.

It has been said that authentic surcharged stamps bear their surcharge on a higher value. This is true in general, but it is not absolutely true. The Italian 15 centessimi of 1865 was transformed into a 20 centessimi in 1866. The idea that the counterfeiter loses by such a surcharge is erroneous. If the application of a surcharge of 25 centime on a stamp of 1 franc does not make its use advantageous to the government, it makes it advantageous to the stamp dealer. If the counterfeiter sells for 10 francs a stamp on which he loses 75 centimes, he still makes a handsome profit.

One of the great motives for doubting surcharges was that they were too dear. When $2 is asked for a surcharge giving to a stamp the value of 25 centimes the buyer's instinct makes him defend his purse. The dealer praises the rarity of such stamps. Often they come in quantities later. This makes one skeptical about authentic stamps.

Whose fault is it? It is certain that the commercial value of a stamp has no relation to its face value. Many causes make the difference. I think that in general one should take care not to accept unique specimens in surcharges. A stamp which costs four or five times its monetary value is dear enough.

Surcharges must be studied as carefully as stamps are. Timbrology is the careful study of stamps, and this study comprises the examination of all their details. One is not a collector because one makes lines of small images in a book.

The collector must study the engraving, the printing, the paper, the qualities, the water-marks, the perforations, the color of paper, the color of the printing of stamps and

many other things.   It is only when one is well aquaint-
ed with all these points that one may tell whether a stamp
is authentic or not.

We must do the same with surcharges; seek for their
birth certificates.

One should not confound with surcharges certain cancellations with figures, as in the 1859 series of Venezuela.
These figures are simply numbers of post offices.

The study of all surcharges should be aided by the list
of all those that are known or that have been proposed.

This subject is interesting and should tempt the ardor
of one of the young writers on stamps.   It is not one of
the objects of this manual.

PROOFS.

Many projects, far from having the same value, have
been confounded under the term proofs.   Few collectors
care for them nowadays.   I believe that they should not
be disdained.

The first class of proofs comprises stamps which have
been executed by order of the government before the
adoption of a type, whether they were used or not.   It
comprises also proofs made for issue of certain projected
series.   There are three proofs of the 10 centimes of France
and stamped envelopes of France engraved under the
empire.

There are a certain number of stamps which were prepared to be used and were withdrawn for various reasons.
One of the best known is that of Connel. He was a director
of the New Brunswick post office.   He had the audacity
to cause his portrait to be engraved on a stamp of the
series of 1860.   He was dismissed for this evidence of
lack of respect for the Queen.

The second class compris es engravers' proofs.   When

a type has been adopted the engraving of it is given to an artist. The latter, in the course of his work is forced to take several proofs. These are generally made in black on China paper. There are proofs of the first French stamps with figures of the Republic, portrait of Napoleon III, etc.

The third class comprises stamps adopted by the government, impressed in color for the purpose of arriving at a choice. Such stamps are carefully printed in order that the qualities of their workmanship may be brought out. Among the known specimens are proofs of Greece and of the original stamps of the United States.

I think that these three classes of proofs are to be recommended to collectors.

There is a fourth class of proofs. When an order has been given to print the stamps, the printer must begin by placing the plate or form in the press and submit it to various trials, the object of which is to place it in the state required to be printed. The printer must verify all the parts of a typographic plate in order that they shall be submitted to an equal pressure. The weak points are to be re-enforced by the addition of small blocks; the color must be of the prescribed shade. For these various operations proofs are made, some of any color, others with the prescribed color, on white or colored sheets and on sheets which have been subjected to one or several impressions. These operations result in innumerable varieties of stamps, the samples of which are found for various issues of stamps of Greece, Spain and Italy. There are not many of them in France, because the government takes care that there should not be.

There is a fifth class of proofs, comprising fanciful impresssions. The distinction from colored proofs is not easily made. The characteristic which is assigned to that class of proofs—that of being proofs of stamps which have been used—is not easily recognized. Nothing prevents an administration from taking the plates of an old series for impression in new colors in view of another issue.   It would be possible to recognize in such a case an impression made with plates more or less worn and not new.   But the proofs, none the less, come under the classification of color proofs.   I can see no reason for a distinction of this class which I include with the third.

There is a sixth class, composed of proposed stamps. Several countries at different epochs have had competitions for stamp designs.

In England when the first postage stamp was adopted in 1839, more than two thousand projects were presented. In Belgium, in 1864, nine candidates sent designs in competition. In France, the stamp actually in use representing Commerce and Peace, the work of Sage, won the premium in competition in 1875, over 431 contributions.

There are known only 200 proofs of the 2,000 which were offered for the English competition.   I have tried to collect all the designs offered in the French competition of 1875.   When I have not been able to obtain the original designs, I have accepted copies and even photographs.

The designs submitted in competion in recent years have been exhibited, are known and may be distinguished from those submitted to governments by engravers not in competition.   To admit these into a collection demands an attentive selection. But it is better to admit a doubtful design than to reject a good one. Nothing is essential, except to know under what conditions the design was submitted to the authorities.

REPRINTS.

The question whether new stamps are preferable to cancelled ones has been the subject of an interminable controversy.   One of the reasons which provoked it was that governments when pressed for old stamps have made new impressions from old plates.   These impressions are called reprints.

A reprint is a new impression of stamps not current, made by means of the original plates, and the paper, the color and perforation of which are almost similar to those of the first issues.

In this definition are all the characteristics of reprints. In the first place the stamp is not current.   If it were, there would be no necessity for a new impression.   There might be a last impression with differences, but it would be a weak impression.

a. A stamp is distinguished above all things by the design.   Ordinarily the design is the same for all the stamps made from one plate, in countries which know how to multiply a design by one of the processes which I have described.   But there are numerous exceptions in ancient series of stamps, in countries where the art of the engraver has few experienced representatives.   A reprint must therefore reproduce a unique type or many types. The imprint is made from the original plate, otherwise it would be an imitation or a counterfeit, or a photo-engraved reproduction.

b. All the parts of the design have not the same importance.   The portrait, or at least the central figure, must always be identical ; but there are cases where the frame was lacking and had to be replaced.   In such cases the frame furnishes distinctive marks of importance.   This is a secondary point, but it should be noted.

c. The legend which accompanies the design is often formed by movable blocks that vary with the value of the stamp. It has happened that these movable blocks were not preserved and that they have to be replaced by others. This is only a secondary point, but it may, like the frame, furnish distintive characteristics to reprints; the absence of a dot after a word, a difference in the size of letters, a difference in their spacing.

d. The plates may have been in use for a time more or less long, but the result has always been a wearing out of the plate. Reprints made on these worn out plates have incisions more or less effaced, indication of the disappearance of delicate details. At times the plate could not furnish the same number of blocks as formerly, at times rust had eaten the exterior lines and diminished their thickness.

e. The mode of engraving employed determines the mode of impression—line or typography. If the same plate is used the result must be the same mode of impression. There cannot be doubt about this. Formerly lithographic reprints were unknown. Since a few years they are quite common. They are easily recognized. Some are striped with oblique lines, done purposely, in order that they may not be used again. On others the figures had to be made over and this entailed a change in the form, in the size, or a different arrangement of certain details of the design. Repeated impressions may make these differences disappear.

f. The paper used for reprints should have always been the same as that used for the original, but it has not always been. Postal administrations have matched the paper as nearly as they could, but many circumstances have made the thickness, the strength and the tint of paper vary.

It is very difficult to match paper.   Water-marks have been abandoned or Dickinson threads have been neglected, or their shades have not been matched.   Paper has been used the water-mark of which is different from that of the original.

g. Colors used in impressions have been necessarily similar.   Black, blue and red have been used wherever these colors were originally employed, but shades have been neglected.   In every country the color of stamps has been preserved, but the shades have varied.   In general the shade of a stamp reproduces that of the corresponding stamp of the series used at the time of the reprint.   Colors of reprints are more vivid than colors of originals and this fact is explained by the use of colors that chemists are improving every day.

If one knows the date of the use of a shade one may tell the date of a reprint.

h. The oldest stamps were not perforated. The presence of a perforation or the absence of a margin serves to distinguish reprints.   Even when the original stamp was perforated, examination of the indentation will almost always furnish distinctive characteristics.   In general, the number of perforations is not the same.   Often the rouletting of reprints is that of the stamps used in the same epoch.

i. Even the reverse of the stamp may furnish indications in reprints.   Certain countries used formerly a coarse and strongly colored material for the gum, dextrine or common gelatine.   The use of a whiter or finer substance serves to establish a distinction.

j.   If the original stamp bore one of several surcharges the reprint will bear preferably the latest surcharge, often modified.

k.   The greater part of the preceding observations is applicable to stamped envelopes; but for these examination of the flap may furnish some information. The gaufered design of the ancient envelopes is not reproduced on the new ones, or the design is the one which was used at the time that the reprint was made.

Many reprints are made not on entire envelopes but on pieces of paper. So, when the latter is laid one may find vertical instead of oblique lines in the paper which prove that the reprint was made on wrappers. Moreover, the arrangement of the gum on the flap of the envelope may furnish a distinctive characteristic. If the gum covers the greater part of the flap the manufacture was recent.

In noticing all these possible differences I have omitted designedly the differences that result from the action of time. These characteristics, appreciable to-day when the reprint is recent, may disappear in years. The characteristics which I have indicated, on the contrary, are permanent and shall be as evident in centuries as they are now.

That is why I have given them.

There is no special characteristic for reprints, but there is, a union of characteristics, and if ordinarily it is more convenient to indicate the most salient of them in every reprint, this is not a reason to neglect the others.

I do not intend to review all the known reprints. Such an enumeration does not enter into the subject of this manual.

Must one collect reprints? I should not be exclusive on this point. I think that a restricted collection should welcome well made reprints for stamps which it is impossible to procure, but should welcome them as reprints. The collector who tries to tell in his work the history of stamps in examples, will do well to welcome reprints, the comparison of which with original stamps will best permit him to make the distinction; but such a collection should comprise only the principal varieties, neglecting all the subtleties which have little significance in reprints.

The more a reprint shall be like an original, the more it should be welcomed.

COUNTERFEIT STAMPS.

The counterfeiter wishes to deceive either the government that issues stamps or the amateurs that collect them.   The first case is not common.   The more care a stamp has required. the more difficult it is to counterfeit it.

Should one collect counterfeit stamps ?   Yes, if one is making a complete collection of stamps; but it is well to note that they are a postal curiosity, interesting only to a restricted number of collectors.

Counterfeit stamps issued to deceive collectors are more common, but there are several varieties of them.   The oldest stamps, the first issued, were issued in limited number, have remained rare and it is extremely difficult to obtain them.   The number of demands for them increasing with the number of collectors, different means have been used to satisfy the latter.   There were reprints made by governments; there were reprints made by dealers, showing differences in paper. water-mark and perforations, but which were not counterfeit stamps.   There were new plates made.   Engraving and mode of impression have often been the same for reprints as for original stamps, though the original plates were not used. but the counterfeits and the original issue are seldom identical.   It is impossible for an artist to reproduce a design, even if it be his own work, without variation.

The proof of this is in the number of sub-types one may find on stamps impressed from a single plate.

The inexperience of collectors aids counterfeiters. This is why certain collections are stuffed with false stamps. But there are counterfeit stamps made by skillful and dangerous artists, that deceive the most authortative experts.

There are cases where counterfeit stamps have been used to fill the place of extremely rare stamps; but if these counterfeits were sold by honest dealers they were sold as fac-similes, as imitations, and bear a note of warning. Senf Bros. issued, a few years ago, a great number of rare stamps—of American newspapers notably—marked as fac-similes, with the word "false."

In general, to distinguish a false stamp from a true one, the most attentive examination is necessary. I have demonstrated that the cancellation proves nothing in itself; that it is not a proof that the stamp was bought at the post office; that it is extremely easy to counterfeit and that all false stamps are cancelled. There is a way of distinguishing them.

In the first place one should examine the mode of engraving and impression. In a great number of cases lithography has been used instead of typography or line engraving because lithography is less costly. The difference is easily perceptible to those who have acquired some experience with stamps. This characteristic will permit one to reject at once a great number of stamps, but it is not applicable to all.

There is, for one accustomed to the collection of stamps, something in their aspect which makes one recognize the fact that such a stamp was not manufactured by its habitual engravers. Who does not know at first sight a stamp printed in England or in America?

After verifying the differences resulting from the use of

a mode of printing other than the original one, one must study the design. Stamps, several varieties of which exist, are well known. When there is only one variety, one must study with a magnifying glass the small details of the design, principally the secondary details, as eyebrows, eyes, curls, shadows, indicated either by horizontal lines or by hatchings. If the design on the stamp be a coat of arms, all the parts of it must be studied successively.

Examination must be made with the strongest magnifying glass. Every collector may obtain this instrument, but he may lack a point of comparison, he may lack the real authentic stamp. The catalogues issued by Moens and Scott furnish this point of comparison. They reproduce in photo-engravings plates which contain a great number of types.

Plates with the stamps of Afghanistan, of Bhopal, of Bolivia first and second issues, of Corientes, of Providence, Hawaii, of the four Annas of English Indies first issue, of Japan. Jhind, Jummoo Cashmere, Mauritius, Nevis, New Caledonia, Sidney, New South Wales, Phillipine Islands, Switzerland 1850, Tasmania and Victoria have been photo-engraved. The reproductions are scrupulously faithful. But it is very difficult to obtain the exact size of a stamp from the photo-engraving of it. There is always a slight diminution in the reproduction.

I shall not conceal from collectors the fact that the examination with a magnifying glass of the details of a design is painful and tiresome. There is another process of examination used by the expert of the Austrian Bank for bank bills. If two bank bills are placed in a stereoscope there shall be only one bill to the observer's view if they are identical; but if there be a difference of any kind in the design there shall be differences forming two bills.

Photography has furnished the means of discovering

frauds in stamps, by enlarging them considerably and rendering by reproduction differences appreciable to the naked eye which were formerly only suspected. Thanks to an ingenious arrangement, invented by Charles de Thierry, stamps of the ordinary size of the French stamp have been transformed into images a yard in height. A stamp may be enlarged 900 times.

Two stamps may be placed side by side for comparison. The enlarged image is projected on a white cloth and may be visible to several persons at once. I have applied this process to the examination of several counterfeit stamps with the following results :

Difference in the size of the stamps.

Difference in their component parts.

Difference in the number and size of the pearls of a crown, of the vertical lines forming a background of gules, modifications of the form of details in a coat of arms, changes in portraits, hair, ears, eyes, mouth, beard.

Modification in the form of certain secondary details in the design, as curve of the shading lines. But in the differences most easily observed the counterfeits were relatively coarse in design.

After examining the details of a design one must examine the details of the legend and figures. One must compare the form of the letters, the arrangement of the inscription, the length of each word and the space between the lines. One may study the figures with relation to their form, their ornament, their shading, the form of the frame in which they are contained. All these differences are easily recognized on stamps which have been enlarged a hundred fold. One may also find characteristic signs, secret marks by which governments distinguish counterfeits.

When the legend is in Roman characters one may distinguish the false from the true inscription.   Yet the en-graver of an authentic stamp may make an error in the legend.   Such a fault, however, is found oftener in coun-terfeit stamps, and principally in those the legend of which is in one of the Oriental languages.

Other characteristics taken from parts of the stamp other than the design, the legend or the mode of impres-sion are of much less value.   The color of a stamp will attract attention; examination with a magnifying glass will confirm or destroy presumption against its authen-ticity.   Paper will furnish also means of verifying this; the absence of a water-mark, the quality of paper, plain or laid, the yellowish color of the tint of the paper will give indications.   The quality of the gum, the rouletting, the perforations, will complete the researches.

A convenient method would be to reproduce in enlarged photographs the true and the false stamps.   The enlarg-ment need not be as considerable as that which I have indicated.   Photographic plates 12x9 centimetres in size would suffice.   They would enlarge at least twenty-five times.   Moreover, a collection formed of all these photo-graphs would make an invaluable reference album.   It has been noticed that the publication of distinctive signs between the true and false stamps has permitted counter-feiters of the latter to correct them.   If a reference album existed there would be no need for descriptions.   Com-parison of false stamps with the photographs of the album would be sufficient.

The first counterfeit stamp that I saw was a so-called Chinese stamp.   It appeared in these values: 3 cent blue, 5 cent red and 10 cent yellow.   Its design represented the American eagle above a Chinaman carrying a parasol and, in a perspective, the porcelain tower of Nankin; in the lower part of the stamp was a vessel.   The names of the four ports open at that epoch to European commerce,

Amoy, Ningpo, Shanghai and Hon-Kong, were printed
on the frame.   At the right were inscriptions, apparently
Chinese.   There was a notice in English saying that the
Anglo-Chinese steamship line possessed four steamers of
from 400 to 500 horse-power.   The stamp was submitted
to the examination of an Oriental scholar who demonstrated that the Chinese signs on the stamp were purely
fantastic.   He said that the first sign reproduced something which resembled the word heaven in Chinese, but
there is no connection between heaven and the post
office; even in China.

In 1873 there were rumors of the adoption of stamps in
in Burmah, and ambassadors from that country visited the
principal states of Europe.   Moens had a series of seven
stamps said to have been issued as local stamps for British Burmah.   They resembled stamps of Cashmere, but
attentive examination revealed in the author of the stamps
a complete ignorance of the numerous characters of the
various languages of India.   The lotos of the upper part
was of Chinese and not Indian origin; the letters placed
underneath represented neither the arms of Burmah nor
its alphabet.   The figures were those in use in Cashmere.

Several dealers of Paris were made the victims of another fraud.   A personage, who wore a fez and posed as
director of a Persian post office submitted stamps of
Cabul.   They represented types similar to those of the
tiger's head, in varied colors, with an addition of ornaments at the angles like those of the real stamps.   The
author had so little knowledge of stamps that he had attributed fantastic values to them.   The values were in
letters above or below the tiger's head.   The counterfeiter was not aware of this and gave other values.   On
envelopes of a country where France had no represen-
tative the words Cabul and post office were written in

French, as if French were the official language of the country.

Until now counterfeiters of Oriental stamps have not been Oriental scholars, but the Chinese and Japanese engravers have produced counterfeits of Chinese and Japanese stamps with marvellous skillfulness.

At the beginning of 1867 there were sold in England two 1 real stamps, one black and one blue, represented to have been issued at Salvador. These stamps were badly printed. Soon after, the issue of a real series engraved by the American Bank Note Company was announced.

There are to be noted counterfeit Sobre-porte stamps of Colombia. In 1868 there appeared a red stamp said to be of Paraguay, representing a steamer in an oval and recalling the stamps of the Suez Canal and of Santa Lucia. This stamp, the design of which was incorrect and the legends of which were irregular, seemed doubtful because Paraguay was then struggling against Brazil. This was not the only counterfeit stamp of Paraguay. There was a counterfeit series of three stamps in 1866, a counterfeit series of two stamps in 1891 and the Impresos in 1892.

In fine, in counterfeit stamps there are multiple characteristics, there is not a single characteristic. One needs a patient and profound study of stamps in their details and a great deal of experience. The question of counterfeit stamps is one of those that preoccupy collectors and societies the most. Therefore, we are not surprised by the announcement that the London society has appointed a committee composed of men of indisputable authority, intrusted with the mission to distinguish the really good imitations from the dangerous frauds which have been issued and sold as rare and valuable stamps. The committee will form a sort of registering office, a real stud book for stamps, wherein one shall be able to verify the pedigree of every valuable stamp.

I approve this resolution and hope that it will be imitated in France. To distinguish false from authentic surcharges it will be sufficient to refer to what I have said in the preceding chapter on the legends of stamps printed in Roman characters.

UNIVERSAL POSTAL UNION.

The idea of extending to all countries of the world the principles of receprocity prevailing to-day in the administration of the post offices of every country, is not new. In May, 1863, at the instigation of the United States, a meeting of delegates discussed for a month in Paris the rules which were to govern postal traffic and the relations of governments to one another. The result of this conference was a declaration of principles, without binding character But these principles passed rapidly from theory into practice and prepared the way for the constitution of the Universal Postal Union.

Negotiations were begun among the principal states of Europe and the United States of America. A meeting of delegates at Berne was decided upon. The congress t ok as a basis for its deliberations the propositions formulated by the administration of the German post office. There was formed a union of Germany, Austria-Hungary, Belgium, Denmark, Egypt, Spain, United States of America, France, Great Britain, Greece, Italy, Luxembourg, Norway, Netherlands, Portugal, Roumania, Russia, Servia, Sweden, Switzerland and Turkey. The principal conditions of the union were as follows:

Art. I.—The countries among which the present treaty is concluded shall form, under the designation of General Postal Union, a single postal territory for the exchange of correspondence among their post offices.

Art. II.—The stipulations of this treaty shall be extended to letters, post cards, books, newspapers and other printed matter, samples of merchandise and business papers coming from one of the countries of the union and destined for another of these countries.

ART. III.—The duty shall be 25 centimes per letter. As a temporary measure the tax may be increased to 32 centimes or decreased to 20 centimes. The weight of a single letter shall be 15 grammes. The tax on letters above this weight shall be the usual rate on each additional 15 grammes or fraction thereof. Letters not stamped in advance shall be charged for twice. Post cards must be stamped in advance. Maritime transport for more than 300 miles shall be subjected to a surtax of half the general tax.

ART. IV.—The tax on printed matter, business papers and samples, shall be fixed at 7 centimes, but may be raised to 11 or lowered to five centimes. The increase in price shall be figured by each fifty grammes or fraction of fifty grammes. Maximum weight: 250 grammes for samples and 1000 grammes for the rest.

ART. V.—Taxes for registry shall be those of the country where registered. In case of loss there shall be an indemnity of 50 francs.

ART. VI.—Postage shall be paid by means of postage stamp or stamped envelope. Newspapers or printed matter not stamped will not be forwarded.

ART. VII.—Returns of letters are made without charge.

ART. VIII.—Official letters of the post offices are postage free.

ART. IX.—Each administration retains the amount of duty that it has charged.

ART. X.—A transit tax is accorded as a compensation to countries serving as intermediaries, by their geographical situation and by the means at their disposition. A country which has no interest in attracting the transit would perhaps refuse to take it.

Art. XI.—Is relative to countries not in the union.

Art. XII.—Letters, the value of which is declared, and money orders shall be the object of future arrangements.

Arts. XIII and XIV.—Contain arrangements for applications of the treaty.

Art. XV.—Creates an international bureau of the union at Berne.

Art. XVI.—Regulates the arbitration of disputes.

Art. XVII.—Is relative to the admission of countries which are not in the union.

Art. XVIII.—Decides upon the triennial meeting of the Congress.

Art. XIX.—Treats of the duration of the treaty and of its first application, July 1, 1875.

Art. XX.—Abrogates special treaties not in accordance with the present one.

The treaty was ratified May 3, 1875.

A certain number of other questions were treated by the Congress. One of the first ones, submitted by the delegate from Turkey, related to the suppression of foreign postal agencies. There were propositions made, without success, that in various countries postage stamps of the same value should have the same color, that international postage stamps should be created, and that a system of notices or advertising be allowed on postage stamps.

January 27, 1876, the British Indies and the French colonies, entered the union. New adherents followed: the Argentine Republic, Brazil, the Danish colonies, the Spanish colonies, various English colonies, Canada, Japan, Mexico, Montenegro, Dutch colonies, Peru, Persia, the Portuguese colonies and Salvador.

In 1878, when the Congress met at Paris 31 states were

members of the Postal Union. The discussions of the
delegates resulted in a revision of the articles of the
treaty of Berne and in an improvement of the system.
The Postal Union took the name Universal Postal Union,
which it deserved.

The legend card correspondence was replaced by the
legend post card.

The tax on business paper could not be made lower
than 25 centimes and that of samples could not be made
lower than 10 centimes. Objects could be registered for
a charge of 25 centimes at the maximum, in European
states, and 15 centimes in the other states.

A special arrangement regarding the exchange of let-
ters with declared values was signed among Germany,
Austria-Hungary, Belgium, Denmark, the Danish colonies,
Egypt, France, the French colonies, Italy, Luxembourg,
Norway, Netherlands, Portugal and its colonies, Roum-
ania, Russia, Servia, Sweden and Switzerland.

Another special arrangement concerns the exchange
of money orders among the same countries, except the
Danish and Portuguese colonies, Russia and Servia. The
treaty was signed June 1, 1878 and put into operation
April 1, 1879.

The regulations for the execution of the Convention of
Paris contain a table of the taxes of the union in the
money of every country, for those that do not use the
frank as monetary unit.

The Congress of Lisbon was opened February 4, 1885.
Improvements were made in the service.

It was recommended to place stamps at the upper
right corner of envelopes, but this recommendation was
not obligatory.

The various administrations agreed to aid one another
against counterfeiters.

The creation of a universal stamp was rejected as impracticable.

The proposition to adopt type colors, 5 centimes green, 10 centimes red, 25 centimes blue, was renewed. It was shown that it was already in force in 36 countries. It was decided that it had little advantage for international service and that it might cause confusion among stamps of various countries. The assembly resolved that the use of color types might be made general but it was not obligatory.

It was decided that each country should send to the International Bureau three collections of its stamps instead of one.

The issue of the double post cards was not declared obligatory, but the states that did not use them were required to send back the replies of the countries that used them.

Ratification of the new convention occured April 1, 1886.

The Congress of Vienna was opened May 20, 1891. New states had been admitted since the Congress of Lisbon—Belgian Congo and the Tunis Regency among others—and there were at the meeting representatives of fifty countries.

Uniformity of colors was refused, France opposing the proposition.

Necessary measures to prohibit and repress counterfeiting, sale and distribution of vignettes and stamps in use in postal service, were adopted.

Luxembourg renewed the proposition to make postage stamps universal, at least in the case of stamps of 25 and 5 centimes. These stamps could not be used for exterior postage nor be exchanged for money. The manufacture would be in the care of the central bureau, the sale would be for the benefit of all the countries of the union and, after the deduction of the expenses, the profit would be shared in a proportion to be determined. The United States supported this measure, with the aim to spare travellers the incovenience of changing stamps.   Germany objected to the project because it might create an international money that would cause speculation.

spite of the United States, who proposed to prohibit the sale of such stamps by others than post offices, the proposition was rejected.

It was again decided that vignettes should be placed only on the reverse of cards.

Washington was selected as the place of the future Congress, and the meeting was closed July 4, 1891.

Such are, in brief, the principal measures and the most interesting dicussions from the collector's point of view, of the Congresses of Berne, Paris, Lisbon and Vienna.

There remains for me only to reproduce an interesting table presented at each Congress.   I reproduce it with slight modifications of form and details.

The Monetary Union, which was originally concluded among France, Belgium, Switzerland, Italy and Greece, had for a basis the franc, divided into 100 centimes.   In Switzerland centimes are called rappen, and in Greece lepta. The system was adopted by other states, but the Monetary Union remained limited to the five original states and their colonies.

The other countries which have adopted the franc and centime are:

Luxembourg.

Spain, where the franc—peseta—is divided into four reals, each real valued at 25 centimes.

Tunis.

Servia, where the franc is called dinar and the centime para.

Roumania, where the franc is a leu and the centimes are bany.

Bulgaria, where the lion is the franc and the stotinki are centimes.

Venezuela where the Bolivar is the franc.

COUNTRIES WHERE THE MONETARY UNIT IS NOT THE FRANC.

Countries.	Monetary Unit	Currency	Contra-Centimes 25	Contra-Centimes 10	Contra-Centimes 5
Germany	Reichm'k	Pfennig	20	10	5
United States of America	Dollar	Cents	5	2	1
Argentine Republic	Peso	Centavos	8	4	2
Austria-Hungary	Florin	Kreuzer	10	5	3
Bolivia	Piastre	Centavos	5	2	1
Brazil		Reis	100	50	25
Chili	Piastre	Centavos	5	2	1
Colombia	Peso	Centavos	5	2	1
Costa Rica	Peso	Centavos	5	2	1
Denmark	Krone	Ore	20	10	5
Greenland	Krone	Ore	20	10	5
Danish Colonies					
West Indies	Florin	Cents	5	2	1
San Domingo	Piastre	Centavos	5	2	1
Egypt	Piastre	Paras	40	20	10
Ecuador	Piastre or Sucre	Centavos	5	2	1
Great Britain	Pounds, Shillings	Pence	2½	1	½
Canada	Dollar	Cents	5	2	1
British India	Rupee	Annas	2	¾	½
British Colonies.					
English Guiana, Hong Kong, Labuan, Straits Settlements	Dollar	Cents	5	2	1
Jamaica and West Indies	Pounds Shillings	Pence	2½	1	½
Ceylon	Rupee	Cents	14	5	2½
Mauritius	Rupee	Centimes	10	4	2
Cyprus		Piastres	2	1	½
Guatemala	Peso	Centavos	5	2	1
Hawaii	Dollar	Cents	5	2	1
Honduras	Peso	Centavos	5	2	1
Japan	Yen	Sen	5	2	1
Liberia	Dollar	Cents	5	2	1
Mexico	Piastre	Centavos	6	3	2
Montenegro	Florin	Soldi	10	5	3
Nicaragua	Peso	Centavos	5	2	1
Paraguay	Piastre	Centavos	5	2	1
Netherlands	Florin	Cents	12½	5	1½
Peru	Sol	Centavos	5	2	1
Persia	Kran	Shahis	7	3	1
Portugal and colonies		Reis	50	20	10
Portuguese India		Tanga	2	10 reis	5 reis
Russia	Rouble	Kopecks	7	3	2
Salvador	Peso	Centavos	5	2	1
Siam		Atts	7½	3	1½
Norway and Sweden	Krone	Ore	20	10	5
Turkey	Piastre	Paras	50	20	10
Uruguay	Peso	Centes'os	5	2	1

FORMATION OF AN ALBUM.

In order to complete what I have said about stamps, I must speak of the formation of the album which is to contain their collection.   I think that the novice will do well to select an album already prepared.   In this selection he will find an embarrassment of riches.   He will find in albums a place already indicated for the greatest number of stamps that he may hope to obtain.   If there be place in a blank album to insert sheets for new acquisitions, it will last for years.

If the collector has a great love for stamps, if his study of them leads him to seek for all the varieties that he may hear of, or that he may find himself, a prepared album is insufficient.   The collector has to create one. This is what all serious collectors have done.   As I have done it myself I shall tell the method that I have adopted in my album.

If the collector gathers in his collection all the kinds of stamps that I have written of, he may find my suggestions useful.   The collector of a restricted collection may find in the development of them interesting indications.

CHOICE OF STAMPS.

Begin your collection by gathering a great quantity of stamps.   Ordinarily, family or business relations are the purveyors of stamps, but after you have asked for their contributions in all possible circumstances, you must have recourse to stamp dealers.   It is only after you have gathered hundreds of stamps that you may think of selecting an album.

The stamps which one obtains should be in their best state of preservation.   Nothing is easier when they are new.   There is a choice of modern issues at all stamp shops.   And certainly, it is much preferable to collect new stamps. They are more agreeable to the touch but they are more costly.   Stamps of issues of thirty years ago, stamps which have been in use only for a short time, were generally issued in a limited number.   Their use was not as extended as it has become.   Payment of letter postage in advance was not obligatory, and the slightest statistics demonstrate the considerable difference which time has wrought in the stamp manufacture of all countries.

It is especially since the Congress of Berne and the formation of the Universal Postal Union that internal relations have increased   There are stamps which one cannot obtain in any other form than cancelled.   Happy are those who find them in that condition. There are persons who prefer cancelled stamps because they are less costly.   I do not blame them.   In stamp collecting everybody must act in accordance with his purse.   But cancelled stamps should be selected in their best possible state of preservation.

For the collector the cancellation on stamps must be as little apparent as possible.   It must affect only the frame and the accessory parts of the stamp and leave visible the portrait, the arms and the important parts of the design.

Stamps which it is difficult to obtain must be accepted as they occur.   With a little care one may give them a satisfying air.   One may exchange them sometime without loss, for they retain their value.   It is absolutely necessary that they should not have any alteration in color of print or of paper.

I have shown that cancellation has no value; that it was not a proof that the stamp had been bought at the post office.   The best distinctive signs are in details of design and legend; in processes of engraving or printing; in characteristics furnished by paper and water-marks. Cancellation is not a warrant of authenticity.   It is at best a presumption of authenticity, and then only when its own authenticity has been established.   The first advice to a novice, at all events, is to buy his stamps from honest merchants, even if he has to pay more for them.

PREPARATION OF STAMPS.

After you have made a choice of the stamps which are to figure in your collection, you must dress them.   Formerly all stamps were washed with water.   The process destroyed stamps printed in water colors or on a background easily dissolved in water.   There were people also who used soap to remove cancellations made with greasy ink.   They soon learned that they destroyed the relief of certain stamps and altered their colors.   There were also people who used chemicals.   They should have known that it is indispensable to avoid even a change in the shade of a color.

A rare cancelled stamp is of much greater value than the same stamp washed and repaired.   The repaired stamp has the air of an old man trying to look young with arts of the hairdresser and tailor.

Washed stamps have lost their gum.   The gum is a sign of authenticity. Remove it and the paper becomes soft, the water-mark disappears and the pressure between leaves of blotting paper has effaced indespensable ornaments.   How may one distinguish original stamps from reprints, when the original ornaments have been effaced?

It does not follow that the reverse of a stamp should be kept with all its thicknesses of paper.   To remove these, pressure of the stamp between two blotting paper leaves is sufficient. I do not condemn a slight washing of stamps not gaufered with a fine sponge dipped in pure water.

It is necessary to preserve the gum of stamps; it is necessary to preserve their margins also. To collectors of a limited number of stamps who neglect all the varieties based on the presence or absence of perforations, I shall say that it is a grave fault to cut the margins of stamps or suppress their indentations. I cannot repeat too often that a stamp deprived of one of its characteristics has lost a great deal of its value. What collector may say in advance that he will be always content with a restricted collection and never think of making a scientific one.

Conclusions: 1.—Abstain from all chemical washing of stamps; 2.—Retain the margins of stamps?

MOUNTING OF STAMPS.

Before placing the stamps in the album there are precautions to be taken.

The mounting must have the following advantages :

1. Facility to examine the stamp.
2. Sufficient tenacity.

It is certain that the design of a stamp is its capital part; but the authors of an issue have not contented themselves with the difficulties that the design puts in the way of counterfeiters. The paper often contains an official water-mark. How may one verify it if the stamp is gummed on its mounting.

The first stamp collectors affixed their stamps on the pages of their albums as they would have affixed them on envelopes of their letters, and so they could never verify water-marks. The first catalogues note only the loops and rays in water-marks of the stamps of Spain and of the West Indies from 1855 to 1856. Examination of the water-marks permits one to distinguish certain primitive issues from their reprints. For example, the stamps of Prussia issued in 1850, with a laurel crown, are distinguished by that sign from the same stamps reprinted in 1864.

If one examines a sheet of stamps one remarks that there are in the intervals of the stamps rows of perforations which facilitate their separation.   I have described these perforations in another chapter of this manual.   In order to verify the modes of separation and to count them, the stamp must not be affixed to the album.

I believe that the following system fulfills perfectly the two conditions stated at the beginning of this chapter. It is a system which I have used for years without ever feeling the necessity for its improvement.

Take a band of thin paper measuring eight or ten millimetres in width.   It may be of any length. The stamps are affixed by their lower half on this band.   The band is folded and the folded part is gummed on another sheet of stronger paper.   Then a margin measuring about two millimetres, and regular, is cut around the stamp.   Thus the stamp is mounted on a hinge on strong paper and is easily examined.

I use a solution of gum arabic for all mountings. Mucilage might be used with the same advantage.

MOUNTING OF ENVELOPES AND CARDS.

For the mounting of envelopes and cards the system is different.   The first question is whether envelopes are to be cut or preserved entire.   The partisans of cutting the envelopes say that the stamp and not the paper is the thing to be collected, that the entire envelope occupies much space and thickens the volume, always large, of the album.   Partisans of the other system reply that every stamp must be collected in the form in which it was furnished by the post office, that is, in this case, the entire envelope. Otherwise it is impossible to know if the stamp occupies the flap of the envelope, as in the ancient issues of Russia and Finland, or if it is on the face of the envelope, or if it is at the right or the left of the envelope —important considerations since the issues of certain countries as Hanover, Lubeck and Russia may be distinguished only by whether the stamp is at the right or the left.

When the type of the stamped envelopes is the same as that of the movable stamps, as in Prussia 1861, Lubeck 1863 and Austria 1861, 1863 and 1867, it may be difficult to distinguish both. It may be said that the envelope stamp, ordinarily, is traversed or surmounted by two lines of inscription, and that the movable stamp has not these two lines and is often perforated. However, the excep. tions are numerous enough to embarass the unexperienced collector.

If the entire envelope occupies more space than the separate stamp, in compensation for this the envelope retains all its value and often gains a higher value. There are stamps of Hanover without value when they are separated, that gain a considerable premium when offered with the envelope: for instance the 1 groschen of 1858. Similar instances occur in Prussia and Baden.

When the envelope is entire, its form, the form of the flap, the gaufered design, the disposition of the gum at the edge, permit one to recognize with facility an ancient envelope from its reprint and the several editions of one series.

Therefore I advise the collection of envelopes entire, even in restricted collections. To those who have had the misfortune to cut off the stamps and have not the means or the courage to replace the envelopes, I can only propose the application to stamps of envelopes and cards, the system of mounting for movable stamps. But this system may not be used for entire envelopes.   The two following processes offer the same advantages of fixity and facility for examination.

The first system consists in taking a band of white paper fourteen millimetres in width, folded in its length into two parts of seven millimetres each, forming a hinge. Some collectors affix it to the vertical edge of the envelope opposed to the stamp.   Thus, two or three envelopes placed on the same line cover one another on the parts not stamped.

I think it preferable to affix this band to the lower edge of the envelope.   I use a band measuring 222 millimetres by fourteen, folded in its width, and divide one of the halves into six numbered parts from left to right.   Suppose that the envelopes have the stamp at the left.   The half of the band which is divided into six parts being turned at the top, the first envelope is affixed on the parts numbered 1 and 4, the second on numbers 2 and 5, the third on numbers 3 and 6.   If the envelopes have their stamp at the right, the first envelope is affixed on numbers 3 and 6, the second on numbers 3 and 5 and the third on numbers 1 and 4.   Thus the stamp is always apparent.   The half of the hinge which has not been divided serves to affix the group of envelopes on the leaf. This hinge permits the separate examination of every envelope.

The second system is due to Petritz of Dresden.   It consists in the use of narrow bands one by two centimetres in height, and of the width of the album leaf. Only the ends of the envelope are affixed.

ALBUM LEAVES.

If the collector wishes to make his own album, he may find useful the means that I have put into practice.

The leaves of the album must be movable. The leaf which I use is a card of three paper thicknesses for movable stamps and of four paper thicknesses for cards and envelopes, which are heavier. The size is twenty-one centimetres in height by twenty-five in width.

In order to avoid tracing pencil lines on these leaves, pencil lines which must be erased afterwards, I use a drawing board measuring twenty-nine by thirty-nine centimetres. I place the leaf on the board and trace around it a linear frame, rectangular in shape, the horizontal sides of which conform exactly with the line of a T-square.

The upper line is four centimetres from the upper edge; the lower line is at the same distance. The side lines are two centimetres from the edge of the board. Outside of these four lines I affix bands of white board which frame exactly the leaf of the album. It is important that the interior rectangle should be exact.

Then I trace at a distance of six centimetres from the upper edge, on the two lateral bands, a small horizontal line measuring a half centimetre, and write O at the opposite extremity; then I trace other lines from half centimetre to half centimetre, and number them on each side of the rectangle 2, 4, 6, etc. to 96. In the intervals other lines might be traced bearing intermediate numbers, but I do not do this because it is easy to place the T-square at an equal distance between two lines.

Now take the T-square and make it slide on the left edge of the board. The lower edge of the T-square is on the leaf placed in the rectangular frame. This frame measures twenty-five centimetres in width. There are traced on the rule two points, at the edges of the bands and at a distance of twenty-five centimetres, like the interior of the frame. At two centimetres from the right side a second point is traced and a third point is traced toward the left at a distance of 23 centimetres. These last two are therefore at a distance of twenty-one centimetres apart. There are traced on the rule between these two points forty-two divisions of a half centimetre each. Then this length is divided into seven parts of three centimetres, or six sub-divisions each. The six interior lines and the first of each extremity are marked seven.

The space of twenty-one centimetres is then divided into six spaces, each one of which has seven divisions, or 3½ centimetres. The lines which limit the spaces are numbered 6. By subtracting from each extremity a division or a half a centimetre, the remaining line may be divided into five parts having four centimetres each, the limiting lines of which may be numbered 5. There may be another sub-division into four parts yielding spaces of five centimetres or ten divisions.

The T-square will then bear at each division one of the figures 7, 6, 5 and 4 and on the other points from half centimetre to half centimetre a simple dash.

When the stamps are affixed on the leaf this is done by applying the T-square to the line the two extremities of which are marked O. Suppose there are seven stamps of twenty-three millimetres, mounting included, to be affixed. The top of the first stamp is affixed at the left, near the rule. The two extremities are placed at equal distance from the lower part of the two lines marked 7 which limit the first interval. A little gum having been applied to the mounting of the stamp, it may be made to adhere in an instant. The T-square has been made immovable with a screw in order to insure a perfect alignment. The screw is removed, the T-square is lifted and applied on each side at number 14. The interval from o to 14 represents a height of 3½ centimetres. This permits a space between rows of about one centimetre. The whole work is done by fixing the rule successively on numbers 28, 42, 56, 70 and 84. This yields seven rows of seven stamps, or for forty-nine stamps.

If rows of 6, 5 or 4 stamps are to be made, it is sufficient to place the T-square on the corresponding lines.

Between the upper edge of the leaf and the line marked o is a space wherein I inscribe:

1. The kind of stamp, postal, telegraph or revenue.

2. The date of issue.

3. The peculiarities of the stamps with regard to paper, water-mark and perforation.

4. Errors, etc.

Each album leaf thus prepared must contain only one issue and only one species of stamps. It is necessary to retain empty spaces for stamps which one might find later and which are useful to the collector. Proofs and reprints must be placed on following sheets or leaves.

All the stamps of a country having been placed on the leaf without ornaments nor flourishes, but with the greatest regularity, they are preceded by a blank leaf framed in colors. At the top is the name of the country, in the middle is the coat of arms, at the lower edge are the dates of reigns and governments. The flag of the country shows well above the name.

METHOD OF BINDING.

When the stamps are mounted on the leaves it is time to be preoccupied by their binding. I have always found the bindings of leaves too rigid. Bands of canvas or of pasteboard have always been used. I prefer paper bind-

ings.   I use a yellowish paper measuring thirty centimetres in length by six and a half to eight centimetres in
width.   I fold it so that one side will measure one-half
centimetre more than the other.   To apply this binding
I prepare a rectangular frame measuring thirty-one centimetres in height by twenty-seven and one-half in
width.

The edges of the leaf being applied to three sides of the
frame the interior edge of the fourth side of the leaf is
covered with gum.   The wider side of the fold is placed
under the leaf.   A slight pressure will make the leaf adhere to the two sides of the binding.

Two holes are punched in the binding for the thread
which unites the leaves.   In order to insure regularity I
have placed on the sides of the frame four small pieces of
thick cardboard at a distance of four centimetres from the
upper and lower sides, and two other pieces of cardboard
on the upper and lower sides, then applied successfully
the T-square and traced with a pencil on the binding the
places where the holes were to be punched.

THE ALBUM.

When a certain number of leaves of one country have
been gathered they are united by means of round wires
mounted on flat pieces.   A sheet covered with a leaf of
marbled paper gives the air of a book to the united leaves.
A pasteboard box measuring 32x30 centimetres, having a
rounded back in the form of a book, may be marked and
placed in the library like a book.   It is by dint of much
work that I have arrived at this result in album making.
The Maury system is heavy and augments the weight of
each album.   But there are several other experiments
which might be made and mine is only the result of indi-
vidual experience.

❧ FINIS. ❧